HARVESTING PROSPERITY

From Farmer To Agribusiness Mogul

Kenneth Obayuwana

ISBN- 979-888-3737-175

Cover Design: HAPDesigns

Layout and Design by:
Heart2World Publishing
Ago Palace Way. Lagos
w. heart2worldpublishing.org
t. 09056183960
e. heart2worldpublishing@gmail.com

For information on distribution, translation or bulk sales, please contact:
Kenneth Obayuwana

Email: Getwithken@gmail.com

Endorsements

Kenneth Obayuwana has done an outstanding job in sharing a wealth of knowledge in this book. It should be a mandatory textbook for all Agriculture courses in institutions. I love the way he intertwines personal experiences with life's lessons, it is truly commendable. This book will provide invaluable support for beginners and experienced farmers alike, offeringpriceless entrepreneurial insights and soft skills like networking, even if it's at a high cost as one of his experiences indicated.

I commend Kenneth Obayuwana for this valuable resource and believe that he will continue to grow and excel in all his future endeavours. Well done.

Mrs. Olusola Sowemimo
Founder, Ope Farms

The story of grace isn't the absence of work or a cover to be ignorant. There is the tenancy to assume the successful are lucky rather than see the work, the failures, and the will not to give up. This is what Kenneth represents, and this book is a journey chronicled.

Farmer Samson Ogbole

Soilless Farm Lab

This book is loaded with real-life success lessons and principles. It's a great read for every young person aspiring to be significant in their field, not just in agriculture. I have known Kenneth in the 'before & after' versions of his personal development story, and I'm glad he has clearly articulated his story to inspire us, especially those who would stumble on this book. In the words of Arch. Margaret B. Idahosa, if you believe it, you will become it. Read this book and revive that dream, get up, get to work, and you too will harvest prosperity.

Chiemezie Ofodum

Life Coach

The book, *Harvesting Prosperity*, reads like a no-holds barred book on the life and journey of the author, Mr. Kenneth Obayuwana, almost like an autobiography. And I enjoyed reading every chapter of this book. Ken is a young man that I have a lot of professional love and respect for. He has such an inspiring vision and alluring passion for agriculture. He talks and writes about the activities in the sector and industry in such a way that you can't help but want to join him. This book tells both the expert and the rookie about the strategies for success in agriculture. It is a fitting literature for students, the agro-academic community, agro-professionals, existing and potential agro-entrepreneurs. Congratulations, Ken!

Mrs Edobong Akpabio
Executive Director, Greenport Nigeria.

I wholeheartedly endorse 'Harvesting Prosperity' by Kenneth Obayuwana. This insightful book provides a compelling roadmap for achieving financial success and personal growth. Obayuwana's wisdom and practical advice make this a must-read for anyone seeking to cultivate prosperity in their life.

Mrs Victoria Madedor
Head Business Development (Agribusiness & FMCG)
Bank of Industry

This resource is an excellent guide for anyone interested in pursuing a career in agriculture. It provides valuable and practical lessons, along with insightful life lessons and actionable steps to help you succeed. I found your personal experiences shared in this resource truly inspiring and unique, giving a different perspective to the story. Kenneth, thank you for sharing youragricultural journey with us. Your work will undoubtedly inspire many people globally, and God willing, your 10-year vision will soon become a reality. Keep up the good work of making a positive difference in the field of agriculture.

Mrs Sola Omolade Adeleye
Founder, House of ceder International Youth Ministry

Harvesting Prosperity is a groundbreaking and insightful guide to navigating the world of agriculture business, specifically tailored to the Nigerian context but can be applied globally.

Kenneth offers a comprehensive roadmap for aspiring farmers, entrepreneurs, and agribusiness enthusiasts, detailing the essential steps to thrive in the industry.

Through personal anecdotes, practical tips, and industry insights, Kenneth demystifies the challenges of farming in Nigeria, emphasizing the importance of strategic planning, innovation, navigating tough seasons, diversifying your skills and talents to generate more income, networking your way to the top and perseverance.

His emphasis on the significance of mentorship underscores the value of learning from experienced professionals to avoid common pitfalls and accelerate success.

One of the book's most compelling aspects is its focus on the global market and opportunities, highlighting the immense potential for exporting Nigerian farm produce. Kenneth provides invaluable guidance on market trends, networking with great minds, international regulations, and export logistics, empowering readers to tap into lucrative opportunities beyond borders.

What sets Harvesting Prosperity apart is its unwavering confidence optimism, and belief in the transformative power of agriculture. Kenneth's passion for farming shines through every page, inspiring readers to embrace the journey towards prosperity with confidence and determination.

As someone deeply invested in Nigeria's agricultural sector, I highly recommend Harvesting Prosperity to anyone seeking to make a meaningful impact in the industry. Whether you're a novice farmer or a seasoned entrepreneur, this book offers invaluable insights and actionable strategies for achieving sustainable success in agriculture business. Get a copy of this book, don't delay.

Mrs. Emem Nwogwugwu
Author of Parent Organizer
Life & Productivity Coach
Project Consultant – LA Pax Life Project

Harvesting Opportunities is a remarkable story of how any agrientrepreneur can navigate their way to success by leveraging their own resources. I encourage you to read this book and apply the life changing lessons from the life and journey of Kenneth.

Mr. Mene Blessing
CEO, Vetsark Limited

Kenneth Obayuwana is one of the few young Agropreneurs who have remained consistent during his University day till date. His commitment in the sector has birthed other youth who today have become experts in the Agricultural sector. I strongly believe this book will help to build New Agricultural Talents across the world I recommend everyone who aspire to go into Agriculture to get this book.

Mr Akin Alabi
Co-founder, Corporate Farmers international.

In this new book by Kenneth Obayuwana, he touches on some salient points which all those aspiring to go into Agribusiness should be aware of before venturing.
1. Get enough experience, training and knowledge. In truth, Agribusiness is a science hinged on strong business skills without which the investor will fail. Passion and

interest alone will not make it happen. This book has strongly emphasized this and must be taken seriously. The danger of not getting proper training, knowledge and experience before venturing into Agribusiness is evident in the numerous failed investments dotting the Nigerian and African landmass in general. Knowledge first the strategy next. This is the best way to succeed in Agribusiness.

2. Agribusiness is capital intensive and requires a lot of liquid cash in hand. The farmer must have enough liquidity in terms of cash to take care of any emergency or unforeseen situation which could ruin the investment. Have enough cash indeed.

3. Before production starts, the end goal must be clearly defined. It simply means, that, there must be a ready, willing and able buyer of your produce immediately your harvest is ready. Not having this in place ahead of production is a recipe for disaster case by post-harvest losses and wastage due to the lack of inadequate storage infrastructure.

The market, must be sorted right from the start before set harvest date. When you put these 3 key points together in proper perspective, they constitute what one can call MBA101 for all those planning to venture into

Agribusiness development and management to meet consumer needs. Kenneth has succinctly broken them down in this new book and I recommend it to aspiring investors looking in this direction in their minds.

Richard Ogundele
CEO JMSF Agribusiness Nigeria
Executive Chairman Greenport Nigeria
Abuja Nigeria.
Richard.ogundele@Jmsfagribusiness.com
Richardogundele@gmail.com
Www.jmsfagribusiness.com
@jmsfagribiz

Kenneth is truly an example of the #BIUExcellence mindset. From his days as a student, his entrepreneurial mindset was obvious and his disruptive thinking shined brightly, making him stand out from the crowd. He pursued agricultural mastery in a world that wanted to relegate farmers to the back seat...but instead, he proudly showed me one his first products, packaged dried fish. That's when we knew he was special. We are proud of his start and know he will keep rising. This book in your hand is a testament to his triumph.

Bishop FEB Idahosa
President, Benson Idahosa University

Dedication

I dedicate this book to every young person striving to make an impact in the agricultural sector. It was your determination that inspired me to write this book, and I sincerely hope it continues to inspire you to persevere until we achieve food security in our nations.

Acknowledgement

I OFFER MY PROFOUND GRATITUDE TO GOD ALMIGHTY FOR THE grace to embark on and complete this endeavor. You are truly the Alpha and Omega. I bear witness that this work is a product of divine inspiration, something that could have been authored by anyone, yet you chose me. I am eternally thankful.

My heartfelt appreciation goes to my mother for the boundless maternal love and unwavering support she has showered upon me. You are the finest mother anyone could ever hope for.

I reserve a special place in my heart for my wife, whose unwavering support has been instrumental in bringing this project to fruition. She toiled tirelessly, dedicating herself to the realization of this book, even taking on the bulk of the typing.

I extend my thanks to my family members, the entire Obayuwana clan, for their constant support and encouragement. Your belief in me has been a tremendous source of strength.

To my pastor, Rev. Osas Obarisiagbon of the Church of God Mission, I am deeply grateful for the seeds of wisdom you've sown. I stand as a product of your words today.

To the one I affectionately refer to as "Daddy," Pastor Efosa Enobakhare, your decision to mentor me from my youthful days has led to this result. To my esteemed elder brother, Rev. Soares Damola, thank you for your words of wisdom and unwavering support.

To all the dedicated members of our team, I appreciate your tireless commitment to bringing this vision to life. May God bless you abundantly.

A special acknowledgment is due to Rev. Chiemezie Ofodum for your meticulous proofreading and valuable feedback, which shed light on the final form of this work.

I extend my heartfelt appreciation to my friends who have stood by my side through thick and thin. Mr. Kingsley Ikponmwosa, Mr. Rupert Ikhuiwu, Mr. Michael Ofumaduadike, and Miss. Sarah Mebine.. Your support to this project has been immense valuable and you all work hard to make sure something great comes out.

To my dear wife and cherished friend, Mrs. Rose-Helen Obayuwana, who has been a remarkable pillar of strength,

I am genuinely at a loss for words. You are simply the best among the best, a true destiny helper.

Lastly, I express my deep gratitude to my amazing brother and publishers, Tobi Adesanya, for turning this dream into a reality.

Content

FOREWORD

M r. Kenneth Obayuwana is a remarkable young man whom I have had the privilege of mentoring. His success story in agriculture, detailed in this book, 'Harvesting Prosperity' is both inspiring and insightful. Kenneth, like many people, did not initially anticipate embarking on a career as an Agribusiness Mogul. Growing up, his aspirations leaned towards pursuing a medical profession. However, as he progressed through life, a profound passion for agriculture emerged, redirecting his professional trajectory.

As the Founder/CEO of Psaltry International Company Limited, a company specializing in processing cassava into various cassava-based products, including starch, flour, glucose, and the first in Africa and the second in the world to produce cassava-based sorbitol, I too found myself transitioning from a background in biochemistry to a prominent role in agriculture.

Kenneth's journey mirrors mine in many ways, which highlights the potential and rewards that agriculture holds. 'Harvesting Prosperity' goes beyond Kenneth's journey from farming to becoming an Agribusiness Mogul. It serves as a practical guide for those interested in the business of agriculture. The book offers valuable insights into securing funding for your agribusiness and provides an effective blueprint that you can follow, all while remaining accessible to readers with diverse professional backgrounds. It also offers insight into the significance of value addition, a crucial strategy to be profitable in agriculture, improve agricultural production, and boost food security. This book dispels outdated notions about farming, illustrating its contemporary and lucrative nature. It stands as a testimony that regardless of one's career aspirations, a fulfilling space can be found within the dynamic field of agriculture.

In a world where the demand for food production is escalating, with a 50% increase in food production needed to feed the global population of about 8 billion, the importance of agriculture cannot be overstated. As Akinwumi Adesina, President of the African Development Bank Group, rightly puts it, 'Nobody drinks oil, but everybody eats food.'

There is no better time to consider agribusiness, and 'Harvesting Prosperity' serves as a comprehensive guide, providing a roadmap for those eager to explore and capitalize on the immense potential within agriculture.

This book is not just for farmers; it is for anyone looking to build wealth through agriculture, regardless of their professional background. It is my hope that Kenneth's journey, as narrated in this book inspires and informs readers about the transformative possibilities within the agricultural sector.

Oluyemisi Iranloye

Founder/CEO, Psaltry International Company Limited

INTRODUCTION

O VER THE PAST FEW YEARS, I'VE BEEN FLOODED WITH many direct messages from people, all asking for the same answers:

"How can I rise to the top as a leader in the agricultural industry?"

"How do I forge unbreakable bonds within this industry?"

"And please, enlighten me on your secret to successful fundraising for agricultural businesses."

Their persistence and genuine curiosity have sparked a fire within me, compelling me to pen this book. So, here we are! Your answers in black and white.

These people reached out to me because they've noticed how I've successfully forged strong bonds in the agricultural industry, gain recognition, and secure funding several times. So, I wrote this book to share my experiences and answer the question of how I achieved it all. My aim is to show that if I can do it, so can you.

In this book, you'll discover the strategies for building strong relationships within the agricultural industry, raising funds for your agricultural businesses, and identifying potential sources of funding. I share the step-by-step processes I undertook to become a global agricultural business consultant. The insights I provide are based on my personal experiences, not on random research or Google searches. These are practical steps that can genuinely help you succeed in the industry.

Another reason why writing this book became a must, is my unending desire to motivate many young people to join the agricultural industry. It's a massive sector that plays an important role in feeding the world's population. With an annual worth of over 3 billion dollars, the agricultural industry stands as one of the largest industries globally.

According to the United Nations Food and Agricultural Organizations, by 2050, the world will need to produce 50% more food to feed an estimated population of 9.7 billion people. This increase in demand will create opportunities for skilled professionals within the agricultural industry.

In the United States alone, the agricultural sector supports more than 22 million jobs, including farming and related occupations. This highly innovative sector continually develops new technologies and practices to enhance efficiency, sustainability, and profitability. As a result, there are ample opportunities for young individuals to engage and make a positive impact.

The significance of the agricultural industry lies in its contribution to food security. By working in this field, young people can play a critical role in ensuring global access to safe nutrition and affordable food. Many people ask me about the role young individuals can play, and through this book, I aim to demonstrate how, as a young person myself, I have gained relevance in the sector. It serves as motivation for other young individuals to pursue their dreams in agriculture.

Agriculture serves as the backbone of many African economies, accounting for over 50% of the continent's GDP. Approximately 60% of Africa's population is involved in some form of agriculture, making it a vital source of employment and income. Africa possesses 60% of uncultivated land, presenting abundant opportunities for agricultural development and expansion. Agriculture is the largest employer in Africa, providing jobs to over 30% of the population. Nigeria, in particular, relies on the agricultural sector, which contributes over 20% to the country's GDP. This industry holds tremendous potential for youth employment and growth.

I hope that reading this book inspires young people to enter the agricultural sector and discover their own unique roles within it. It is an industry filled with promise, offering countless opportunities for you as a young individual.

Enjoy the journey!

Kenneth Obayuwana

Where it all
STARTED

Chapter One

"Adventure is worthwhile in itself."
— Amelia Earhart

GROWING UP, I DREAMT OF DONNING A WHITE COAT and saving lives as a medical doctor—just like my parents wished for me. With hopes high, I embarked on the arduous journey of exams and applications, braving the storm of JAMB and WASSCE, while applying to renowned universities like the University of Nigeria, Nsukka, and Lagos State University. To broaden my options, I even threw in applications to Federal Polytechnic Auchi and Yaba College of Technology. Little did I know that fate had a twist in store for me, steering me away from the traditional medical field.

As the acceptance letters rolled in, disappointment struck when my dreams of attending the University of Nigeria,

Nsukka, or Lagos State University were shattered. In an unexpected turn, it was Federal Polytechnic, Auchi that offered me admission into Science Laboratory Technology—a course along the medical spectrum. Although it wasn't precisely what I had envisioned, I resolved to embrace the opportunity that had presented itself. After all, Federal Polytechnic, Auchi, chose me among all the schools I had applied to, and my yearning to be part of the medical world could still find its niche here.

My time at Federal Polytechnic, Auchi, became an extraordinary chapter of my life, where I crossed paths with remarkable individuals who shared my values and harboured dreams of greatness. Immersed in a sea of aspiring minds, we fueled each other's ambitions and encouraged one another to reach for the stars. Throughout my academic pursuits, I embarked on a four-month internship at Irowa Medical Centre, an experience that broadened my horizons even further.

Within the walls of Irowa medical centre, I encountered fellow students from different institutions like the University of Benin and Delta State University. Engaging with these remarkable peers from different backgrounds and fields opened my eyes to life's possibilities.

After the completion of my internship, I returned to Federal Polytechnic, Auchi, with a newfound determination to complete my program. The experiences and connections I had built along the way continued to shape my perspective, nudging me closer to a destiny I was only beginning to unravel.

Little did I know that this seemingly divergent path would ultimately lead me to the world of agribusiness—the place where my true passion and purpose would bloom and blossom.

In 2013, I graduated from Federal Polytechnic, Auchi. With diploma in hand, I was full of anticipation and confident that doors of opportunity would swing wide open before me. As days turned into weeks and weeks into a full month, I eagerly awaited my first job offer. Fate smiled upon me when, at long last, an opportunity knocked on my door—a job offer from none other than Ojemai Farms.

Ojemai Farms, as at the time I worked there, stood tall as the fifth largest farm in Nigeria, commanded respect within the industry. Their operations spanned crop farming, animal husbandry, and processing, forming a powerful agricultural combination. Although I might have preferred a role in crop farming or animal farming division, I believe destiny had other plans in store. I was assigned to the processing unit where the magic of transformation —that's where I saw all the magic happen.

The vibrant atmosphere of Ojemai Farm's processing unit became my newfound workspace. I was happy to have my first job right out of school. Surrounded by buzzing machinery and the intoxicating aroma of fresh produce, I knew I was in the right place. Each day presented new challenges and opportunities to learn, as I witnessed firsthand the intricate process of turning raw agricultural materials into refined products.

Right there in the processing unit, we processed 4500 poultry birds daily. We supplied the largest eateries in south-south region (Edo, Delta and Port Harcourt) and some airlines in Nigeria. I felt fulfilled knowing that the work I was doing was providing the products to fuel other industries. The joy of knowing that passengers on an airplane or customers in an eatery will be satisfied by the chickens I processed, gave me a lot of satisfaction. This was how my journey into agribusiness started.

I soaked up knowledge about the entire farm process while I worked there. I also saw that the business was lucrative. Since we processed 4500 birds daily, in my head, I did a calculation on how much the owners of the farm were generating. The results of my findings got me more excited.

From the efficient killing unit to the expertly crafted dressing unit and the maintained cold room, every aspect of the business was excellent. My role found me stationed in the defeathering unit, where I oversaw a dedicated team responsible for delicately removing feathers from the birds. I also had the privilege of supervising the skilled staff who carefully and skillfully sliced the chickens into perfectly portioned parts. The precision and attention to detail were awe-inspiring, leaving no room for error.

Without a doubt, my love for agriculture and agribusiness grew in leaps and bound while working in Ojemai Farm. The more I worked there, the more my passion and interest grew. I also saw the many opportunities in the sector.

I find it amusing how life plays out differently than we thought. Life is full of pivots; Kairos moments that keep shifting us at different times to get us where ought to be. First, I pivoted from my desire to become a Medical Doctor, to studying Science Lab Tech.

Every step we take is a build-up to the next level. I saw my journey as a stepping stone to what was to come. The fact that I was open to every opportunity that came my way even in a course that I didn't want. This openness to opportunities and seeing the possibilities in my environment, opened me up to this new found love in agriculture.

LIFE LESSONS

- Be open to opportunities. Make a commitment to maximise every phase of your life. You may not get what you want or desire at first try, but stay committed to being the best and seizing every moment. You never know if what you do with what you have and where you are, will be the exact stepping stone to that which you truly need.

- Wherever you are working be observant and be willing to learn.

Follow Your Dreams!
Follow Your Passion!

Chapter Two

Wherever your dreams take you, know that this is
precisely where the universe needs you to be.

As with all beginnings, there comes an end. I thoroughly enjoyed my work at Ojemai farms, but I couldn't shake the "What next?" question from my heart. I yearned for more and I knew that there was more for me out there. I finally found the answer to that question and I quit the job happily in 2014.

I left Ojemai farm to Lagos in search of a greener pasture and I resumed with one of the leading bottle water factories called Voltic Water. I was with them for a period nine months. It didn't take me long to again realise that I couldn't continue on this path. I needed to be equipped with more knowledge and competence for the future I believe awaited me. I decided to pursue a Bachelor's degree. I again resigned and returned to Benin City where I went on to volunteer with the Christian Fellowship International (CFI), head office.

My interactions with the incredible men and women at CFI gave me all the push I needed to further my education. I recall my Boss Rev Chiemezie Ofodum will always lit us up with inspiring words firing us to action. He'd often say to us, "If you are a O'level holder go get a B.sc, and if you are a B.sc holder go get an M.sc, if you are an OND holder go get your HND or B.sc degree." I didn't have to think too long and deep on what course to enroll for. I naturally settled for Agriculture.

To aid my quest for this new degree, I secured a partial scholarship at the Benson Idahosa University. BIU, located in Benin City, was—and still is—one of the leading universities in Nigeria founded by Archbishop Benson Andrew Idahosa. I enrolled to study Agronomy. It was a dream come true.

Follow Your Dreams

I am a staunch advocate of the mantra "Follow your dream, follow your passion." I firmly believe in chasing your dreams and working diligently to bring them to fruition. That's the essence of who I am, the type of person I am, and the foundation of my beliefs.

I'm well aware that some people argue against following one's passion, suggesting that it may not always lead to financial success. However, I align myself with the school of thought that ardently states, "Follow your dreams, follow your passions." Pursue them relentlessly, and the rewards will eventually manifest. I champion this agenda because of my personal journey.

At Benson Idahosa University, I strolled into the administrative office on the very first day and secured my admission. At that point, I believed that all universities were essentially the same, whether private or public. I had previously attended a public institution, Federal Polytechnic, Auchi, and my mindset remained largely unchanged. However, that day brought some startling revelations.

While I was at the university, I overheard a conversation between an individual and the administrative staff about the provision of food for students. To my astonishment, I discovered that the university did not provide meals for students; they were required to purchase their own food. This revelation caught me off guard. I was faced with the prospect of buying my own meals every day for the next four to five years, both morning and evening. I was bewildered.

The admission letter I held indicated a program duration of four to five years, but I didn't fully comprehend its implications. When I inquired about it, the response was that my program was five years in duration, but I would likely graduate in four to five years. The tuition fees, however, were calculated based on the full five years. This revelation was my second shock.

When I returned home and had to break the news to my mother, I struggled to find the right words. Her reaction was deeply emotional; she wept, and her tears persisted for days. She would repeatedly express her disbelief, saying, "So, your plan is to study agriculture, to farm, for five years?" She questioned my choice, suggesting I could have pursued other courses. She viewed my decision to study agriculture in a private university as an unconventional and, in her eyes, impractical choice.

During our discussions, my mother would comment, "Why not choose a different course?" She even joked that if she had known I would pursue farming out of passion, she could have sent me to our grandparents to work on their farm all those years. She expressed concerns about how to explain my course of study to her friends, especially when I was enrolled in Agronomy, a course she struggled to pronounce.

I vividly remember conducting Google searches to understand what Agronomy entailed and its potential career prospects. I reassured my mother that she could simply inform her friends that I was studying a course that could lead to employment in pharmaceutical or oil companies, even though I wasn't entirely certain about the accuracy of this information. This explanation seemed to ease her worries, as she believed it was related to medicine and the oil industry.

In essence, I was relentlessly pursuing my dream, which was deeply rooted in my passion for agriculture and the desire to address issues related to hunger and food security. Over the years, despite initial discomfort within my family, particularly from my mother, I continued to follow my dream and passion.

As I progressed on my journey and achieved significant milestones, including winning grants, receiving awards, and gaining recognition for my agricultural pursuits, my family's perspective began to shift. They became more accepting and supportive, especially when they witnessed the impact of my work. My mother, who had initially been ashamed to tell her friends about my course of study, now proudly shared stories of my achievements.

I had the option to study education, a field in which my mother excelled as an educator. There were numerous other courses I could have chosen. However, I remained steadfast in my decision to study agriculture because it aligned with my passion and dreams.

When I resumed in Benson Idahosa University, I was told cooking wasn't permitted within the school hostel. I began to think of what to do to deal with this new reality. My journey into the field of agriculture was further helped when I began studying Agronomy at Benson Idahosa University. It was there that my quest to unravel the intricacies of the agricultural industry took flight. As I progressed through my academic journey, an important moment came—a moment that led me to transfer into Agricultural Economics and Extension Service during my final year. Rest assured, dear reader, I would share my reasons for this transfer in the later parts of this book.

At this juncture of the book, you will agree with me that my passion for agriculture rings true in this narrative. If you happen to follow my presence on social media platforms, you may have noticed my penchant for crop farming—a love affair that consumes a significant portion of my agricultural pursuits. However, agricultural economics is all-encompassing. It envelops the entire spectrum, including farm management, product marketing, and agribusiness administration. This informed my desire to change my department.

During my study at BIU, we often had a three-month summer holiday. Within these months I made up my mind to intentionally immerse myself in activities that aligned with my passion and aspirations. Learning in the areas of my goals and interests have always been a delight to me.

In 2015, I interned with Okomu Farm. Okomu Farm, in my own opinion, is one of the largest farms in Nigeria. As at the time I worked there, the farm sat on twenty-four thousand (24,000) hectares of land and recently I heard they secured another 20 thousand hectares of land again making them sit on forty-four thousand hectares of land and it is owned by foreigners and I believe that is why the name is among the biggest farm in Nigeria.

In my own opinion the largest farm is in Edo state, Presco palm plantation is sitting on forty-five thousand hectare of land and in 2018 they acquire another twenty hectare of land making total of sixty-five hectare of land, Okomu shares boundary with Michelin and as at the time I worked in Okomu, Michelin was sitting on twenty-two hectares of land.

Although it was a rubber plantation, they are the ones that produced car tyres using the latex from the rubber trees and they ensure they makes life better for their staffs, working in Okomu opened my eyes to another aspect of agriculture. They were into processing of palm oil and started diversifying into rubber farm at the time I came into the farm. Working in Okomu opened my eyes to how vast the agricultural industry is and the possibility in this industry. They have one of the best palm oils in Nigeria and working with them also grew my passion for processing the more, it opened my eyes to how large the palm sector is and I got more excited about agriculture, I was happy that I was studying agriculture. I was fully ready for what was in this agricultural sector and I am excited I am here. This was my second experience in the agricultural world.

You can pursue your dreams too

I share this story to inspire you to continually nurture your own passion and dreams. My mother, who was initially embarrassed by my choice, now encourages her friends to consider sending their children to study agriculture based on the positive outcomes they've witnessed in my life. The central message is not to compel everyone to pursue agriculture but to underscore the importance of pursuing one's dreams and passions.

I never anticipated the transformative power of agriculture in my life. It has opened doors for me around the world, provided recognition, and allowed me to achieve things I had always aspired to but didn't know were attainable. Agriculture has become the key to unlocking numerous opportunities.

I want to convey that for every dream you pursue, there is a reward awaiting you. God has placed that dream within you for a reason, and it burns within you for a purpose. If you persist and follow your dream to the end, you will reap the rewards. While the rewards may not materialise immediately, they are certain to come.

At times, people ask about the practicality of pursuing their dreams, particularly when faced with financial challenges. Here's my advice: While you pursue your dreams, you can engage in activities that generate income to support your dream until the rewards materialise. There is indeed a reward for every dream, so it's crucial to pursue your dreams and follow your passions. Follow them to completion, and you will undoubtedly reap the rewards. When those rewards arrive, they will surpass your expectations.

I never foresaw many of the opportunities and experiences that have come my way. Some of these opportunities were part of my vision, but I didn't realise that agriculture would be the key to unlocking them. Pursuing your dreams and passions holds incredible power. Fulfilling your dreams requires a burning passion and a clear sense of purpose to fuel your ambition.

Your dreams and passions should ignite a fire within you, compelling you to take every necessary step to fulfil them. If your dreams fail to stir your soul or drive you to action, they may not be potent enough. A powerful dream should excite you, filling you with enthusiasm and determination.

Regardless of the challenges you encounter, if your dream burns brightly enough to cause a fire in your soul, it will keep you engaged throughout the journey.

I encourage you to relentlessly pursue your dreams. I've had the privilege of speaking with individuals between the ages of 65 and 75, asking them about their greatest regrets. Surprisingly, for most of them, their regrets aren't related to money. They've accumulated wealth. Instead, their most significant regrets revolve around not pursuing their dreams. They wish they had more time, lamenting that they spent years chasing money with the hope that they'd eventually pursue their dreams. This is one of the driving forces behind my own pursuit of dreams.

There is immense power in pursuing your dreams, and your dreams should be substantial enough to keep you awake at night. When your dreams are sufficiently significant, they will motivate you to work tirelessly and seek ways to bring them to fruition. They will keep you awake, driving you to discover the 'how' to turn them into reality. While finding the 'how' may pose challenges, the rewards of realising your dreams far exceed the pursuit of money.

I firmly believe in the pursuit of dreams and persevering until you achieve them.

LIFE LESSONS

- Follow your dreams and the reward will come.

- I have come to realise that in life there is a joy that comes with fulfilling your dream.

- Don't sell your dream for money

I fell in love with
FARMING

Chapter Three

Wherever your dreams take you, know that this is
precisely where the universe needs you to be.

In earlier chapters, I mentioned that at the Benson
Idahosa University, students were not allowed to
prepare their own meals within the hostel. We had
to order food from the cafeteria or eat at the different
restaurants on campus. This meant I had to buy food daily
for a period of 5 years. This was going to cost more and
was a total change of plans than I had. I had previously
thought that I'd get food stuff from home which I could
prepare for myself while on campus. I reckoned that this
would be cheaper. With the high cost of feeding, I knew
I had to do something to make more money and remain
financially buoyant on campus.

In comes Kenneth the Entrepreneur! I immediately switched to business mode. I began to seek and pray for the right ideas that could change my financial fortune. I strongly desired to be financially independent so that I could ease off the burden on my mum who had to shoulder most of the bills of myself and siblings.

In the process, I thought of offering one service or the other that the university could pay me for. So, I reached out to the Deputy Vice-Chancellor Prof Sam Guobadia at the time, who is today the Vice Chancellor (as at the time of this writing). I shared my thoughts on the kinds of solutions I could bring to the school. I suggested to him that I could provide fumigation services, produce liquid soap, and a host of other things.

He noticed the fiery passion I had to solve problems and do business. He then referred me to Mrs. Asemota who, at the time, was in charge of the school's entrepreneurship program. I met Mrs. Asemota and soon became friends, she became the 'go to' person for me. Weeks later, I came up with an idea in the line of fashion. This new idea would require that I move from one room to another within the school hostel to sell the clothes. This was a step in the right direction. I set up a meeting with Mrs. Asemota where I shared the vision with her. Before this meeting, I had informed her of my desire to facilitate one of the sessions during the entrepreneurship program (ENT program).

My goal was to teach people how to make liquid soap, detergent, insecticide, etc. but I was in 100l and it was a 300l course so I could not take it then. When I shared the idea with her, she loved it and she gave me a shop and asked me to keep record of my profit.

Rather than selling from one room to another in the hostel, I was able to set up my own boutique with some money I overpaid in my school fees in the last session.

I named the boutique K-Bax Outfits. With N70,000 in total I went to the market happily to get the goods I needed to sell. I called a painter who did a nice job painting the shop and an electrician did some electrical fittings. In no time, the shop looked like a proper boutique and the goods I had bought at the Onitsha market were sitting comfortably on the shelves in the store.

This was not a walk in the park. Rather than support and encouragement from my peers, a lot of them mocked me but I never felt ashamed. As I write this, I recall vividly the day I opened the shop for sales. I donned my shorts and with several printed flyers in my hands, I went from one place to another telling everyone who cared to listen that I had just opened a boutique on campus.

In the first week I sold goods worth N20,000 (approximately $30). In the second week I sold goods worth N50,000 (approximately $70) and by the third week I had sold more than N70,000 (about $100) worth of goods. This meant that I recovered my capital in the third week and broke even.

The business looked very lucrative to me especially because it was near the girls' hostel and I got the highest patronage from them. It was a unisex store where I sold wares for the ladies and guys. I received payment in cash and also gave some persons credit, who often paid at the end of the month. I made a lot of money here. I consider this a worthy and notable experience in the world of business.

My initial intention wasn't to delve into fashion for the long haul. Rather, it was to leverage fashion as a means to raise capital that could be invested in the agricultural sector. Agriculture, as I was well aware, required substantial capital investment. I was just as interested in making impact as I was about doing business. So, in 2011, I established an NGO called Positive Impact Initiative, which has now evolved into Positive Impact Africa but establish it in BIU in year 2017.

During one of our meetings at the Faculty of Social and Management Science, I noticed that the school's fish pond stood empty. A thought travelled into my mind that very day suggesting that I could utilise the fish pond for rearing catfish. Excited by the opportunity, I stood by the pond for a few moments, contemplating the potential it held. However, I became a little jittery at the very thought of what it would take and what could happen if I requested for the use of the pond, especially considering the shop space the school had granted me for my boutique. But I resolved to cast aside my fears and summon the courage to write a letter to the Dean of my faculty, who was responsible for overseeing the pond's management.

To my delight, the Dean, Prof Molindo responded with enthusiasm, expressing that this was precisely the kind of entrepreneurial spirit the school sought to nurture in its students. With the dean's gracious approval, I swiftly utilised the funds I had saved from my boutique to stock the pond. Before stocking the pond, I undertook necessary maintenance work as it had been neglected for quite some time. And so, my journey into full-time farming began. I was uber-excited. Dreams do come true.

This experience marked a significant milestone for me. I was no longer working under the supervision of others; this time, I was operating my very own farm. As with any new endeavour, I made many mistakes along the way, ones that I now hope you can learn from.

First Mistake: I didn't have a mentor; someone who had done it before and was successful in the catfish business.

Second Mistake: I never knew catfishes fell into the category of carnivores; they could literally eat themselves. This revelation took me by surprise. It underscores the importance of having a mentor by your side. If only I had one, they would have enlightened me about this peculiar behavior. Despite my agricultural background, I realised that practical experience from a seasoned mentor was indispensable.

Allow me to impart this vital lesson to you: in the realm of agribusiness, having a mentor who willingly shares their wisdom is crucial. The agribusiness landscape is far from easy, but fortunately, you are reading this book, equipping yourself with valuable insights at this very moment. It wasn't until after I had stocked 3000 fingerlings that I sought out a mentor.

By that point, I had already endured numerous challenges that a knowledgeable guide could have spared me from. At that time, I turned to Bishop Dickson Ogbahon, a highly knowledgeable figure in the field of agriculture, particularly in this specific domain, to become my mentor. He was genuinely thrilled to see my endeavours and eagerly embraced the opportunity to guide me. Many of the secrets and strategies I employ in my own farming business today, were passed down to me through his mentorship. These invaluable insights cannot be obtained through a simple Google search. People actually pay me for consulting services based on these personal experiences.

I vividly recall one particular visit Bishop Ogbahon made to my farm. He imparted an invaluable piece of advice: "You should not have stocked 3000 fingerlings; you should have just stocked 500 only." He explained that by stocking fewer fingerlings and ensuring they were adequately nourished, they would grow better and be better nourished. This insight came from years of experience in fish farming. It challenged the conventional belief that stocking more fish automatically translates to higher profits.

In reality, the key lies in stocking a modest number and providing them with ample nutrition. This approach exerts pressure on the weight of each fish, increasing it from 1kg to 2kg. With the right market in place, these larger-sized fish can be sold at a premium, yielding substantial returns.

LIFE LESSONS

- Get Experience: In agriculture, practical experience is essential, not just theoretical knowledge. Find someone with hands-on expertise through mentorship, consultancy, or coaching. Experience means having gone through the challenges and successes, providing valuable guidance to avoid costly mistakes. Practical experience is the key to success in agriculture.

- Have Enough Cash: You must have adequate cash before you go into agriculture. In as much as agriculture is lucrative, it is also very capital intensive.

- Secure Your Market: Before you venture into farming, have a ready market for your produce.

- Learn to diversify

- Your experience is another person's light. Learn to document your experience to help others.

Harnessing
OPPORTUNITIES

Chapter Four

"All I knew is that I never wanted to be average."
-Michael Jordan

When I started selling my catfish, I realised a lot of them were too light, weighing below 1kg. This was a big loss for me because I couldn't afford to feed them properly. But then I remembered something from an agricultural seminar I attended where we were taught about agricultural exports and processing. At that same seminar, I made a very important contact with a woman who was into catfish processing.

By now, you must be aware that agribusiness is not just about producing agricultural goods. It also involves processing and adding value to them. I decided to explore catfish processing as a solution. Processing means turning the fish into fillets, smoking them, or freezing them. These processed catfish can be sold at higher prices and even exported, opening up new markets and increasing profits.

By venturing into catfish processing, I not only solved the problem of underweight fish but also discovered a new aspect of agribusiness. Processing added value to my products and attracted more customers. It was a game-changer for my business.

At this point, let me define this word you've come across over and over again; agribusiness.

What is Agribusiness?

According to Oxford Advanced Learners Dictionary "Agribusiness is an industry concerned with the production and sale of farm produce especially involving large companies".

According to Merriam–Webster dictionary "Agribusiness is an industry engaged in the producing operation of farm, the manufacture and distribution of farm equipment and supplies and the processing, storage and distribution of farm commodities.

Simple defined, agribusiness as "the business side of agriculture."

Having defined agribusiness, we may now begin some business side of agriculture that I ventured.

In that seminar, the woman I met gave me her complimentary card. When I started making losses with the catfish business, I quickly searched for her complimentary card and gave her a call. She gave me an estimated cost on the catfish processing and I went for it. I must say, I earned a lot of money processing my catfish. This was my first agribusiness outside catfish farming.

That same 2017, Purple Foundation came to my school for their annual conference tagged "The Empowerment Network" one of the guest speakers, Mr Leonard Ebute spoke on "business Philosophy and Strategy". He spoke on some business strategy; he also spoke on these four crops: 1. Soya bean 2. Cassava (starch) 3. Fresh vegetable and 4. Irish potato.

The speaker emphasised the importance of focusing on a specific crop and exploring its value chains. After attending this conference my perspective shifted. Inspired by this, I began to research on the value chain of cassava and was amazed by what I discovered. It became clear to me that cassava held great potential for value-added products.

Following the advice of one of my mentors to "stay close to the business I wanted to build," I decided to start with cassava farming. I reached out to my elder brother, who had available land, and together we planted cassava, plantain, and pineapple. The following year, it was time to harvest the cassava tubers. Initially, I had plans to enter the lucrative cassava starch industry, but financial constraints led me to consider selling the tubers instead.

I began searching for buyers, but the prices they offered were disappointingly low, selling it at such a price would have resulted in a loss. Then I remembered someone I had met at yet another agriculture-related conference. The lady specialised in processing various types of flour, including cassava flour. It struck me that I could utilise her factory facility to process my cassava tubers into high-quality cassava flour. I placed a call to her and we came to an agreement. That one conversation and the action I took thereafter, led to the birth and repacking of my flour in attractive 1kg packs and branded as Baxto Odourless Fufu. Do you see why it's important to attend industry related events and to network?

To my surprise, I discovered that I made more profit from value-added packaging than from selling the raw tubers. Processing nine tubers of cassava yielded the same income as selling an entire bag of unprocessed cassava. That's a huge difference, if you ask me. This realization opened my eyes to the wealth potential of value additions in agriculture.

With my catfish branded as Baxto Dried Catfish and the cassava flour as Baxto Odourless Fufu, my business gained momentum. I even secured several grants while still being a student, thanks to the success and appeal of these branded products. It became evident that profitable farming lies not only in cultivation but also in understanding the power of value-added processing.

In the next chapter I am going to tell you how I sold the other crops at the farm and I will share how I raised money for my business through grants. Keep reading!

For now, let's look out for some life lessons from this chapter

LIFE LESSONS

1. Before you enter any industry, you must have proper understanding of the industry, not having proper understanding may cost you much.

2. You must understand the value chain of the industry you want to play in and choose the one you are most favourably disposed to. Every industry has a value chain. For example, real estate has a value chain of over 52 different areas. The agriculture industry has over 250 different areas. My advice for you is to pick one crop and extensively look at the value chain and pick one aspect of the value chains. For example, you can pick cassava and look at the value chain an area to specialise in.

3. Attend events. From my story, the defining moments became a reality because of the people I had met. Event/conferences are vital to your personal development and if you must grow, you must learn to attend relevant industry events.

4. Network at events. When I attend events, I intentionally network with relevant people there. Imagine that I hadn't met with the lady who assisted me with her factory equipment, I'd have missed a great opportunity. If I didn't attend those kinds of events, I would not have been able to do business with her. Networking and connecting with people in your industry is very key to your growth. You must learn to network and connect with people in your industry.

5. I want you to also learn this; for every event I attended I took immediate action on what I learned. In this chapter I shared with you how I attended an event and the speaker mentioned cassava crop and that night I started research about the cassava industry. If you attend any event and there is something you need to act on, please do so immediately. Don't procrastinate.

How I discovered profitable paths in
AGRI-BUSINESS

Chapter Five

"The real voyage of discovery consists not in seeking new landscapes, but in having new eyes."
— Marcel Proust

In my previous chapter, I mentioned that I had
planted plantains on the farm. But let me share another
story with you. Back in 2014, I volunteered for the
Christian Fellowship International head office, which was
the campus fellowship of the Church of God Mission.
Even after I gained admission into BIU, I continued
working with them. During the 2017 JAM (Jesus and
Me) Summit, I was entrusted with heading the business
unit for that particular event. I received extensive training
to ensure I could deliver exceptional results. As expected,
we generated a significant profit that year.

Being the head of the business unit, I had the opportunity
to interact with numerous vendors, many of whom were

based in Edo state since the summit took place there. Establishing strong relationships with these vendors was necessary. Throughout the summit, I engaged with all the vendors, building connections and trust. By the end of the event, I had compiled a database of vendors who participated. I maintained contact with them, recognising the power of numbers in business. Some of these vendors were vendors from BIU, and we continued our friendship in school after the summit.

One day, while chatting with a vendor at the cafeteria, I saw another vendor arriving with two bunches of plantain. Some of the vendors were pleading with him to sell one bunch to them. Curious, I inquired about the situation. They explained that plantains had become scarce, and this sparked an idea within me. I offered to supply them with more affordable plantains, and they eagerly requested my assistance. However, at that time, my own plantains were not yet ready for harvest. Determined to fulfill their request, I hurried to the Okada market the following week to procure the plantains they needed. And so, the journey of supplying plantains to the BIU cafeteria began.

Some vendors purchased as many as five dozen bunches, while others bought six to seven dozen. Word quickly spread among the market women they used to buy from, wondering why their customers had shifted to me. The vendors shared my story, explaining that I supplied directly from the village. Soon enough, the market women reached out to me, requesting that I supply them as well. And so, I expanded my market to include the local market. As I posted updates on Facebook about my plantain venture, people from Lagos began expressing interest, asking if I could supply them too. Without hesitation, I started supplying plantains to customers in Lagos. By the time my own plantains were ready for harvest, I already had a market waiting for them. Selling directly from my farm, I made a substantial amount of money supplying plantains to food vendors across Edo State.

Today, I have assisted numerous Nigerian students in selling plantains to vendors at their respective schools. After I graduated, I officially handed over this business to someone else. I introduced him to the vendors and informed them that he would be their new supplier. Apart from plantains, there are other agro-commodities you can trade and profit from. I have friends who sell pure honey and have made a significant income from it. You can follow a similar path, trading in plantains or exploring other options like honey, eggs, rice, or palm oil.

The key is to find a reliable source for these commodities at affordable prices and identify potential customers to supply. Your local vendors, provision stores, supermarkets, or even festive markets can be excellent targets. Agro-commodities such as rice, honey, and palm oil have a longer shelf life, making them ideal for storage and selling during specific seasons. There are numerous agro-commodities to consider, so take the time to think about which one suits your interests and goals. Assess the costs, calculate potential profits, and start taking action.

Here's a valuable insight: acting as a "middle man" in the agricultural industry, aggregating produce from farmers and selling to the market, can be more lucrative than actual farming. Trust me, there's considerable profit potential in the world of agro-commodities. If you're unfamiliar with the term, agro-commodities are basic agricultural products like maize, yam, plantains, eggs, soybeans, and more. They are everyday essentials in high demand.

Before you trade any agro commodity ensure that agro commodity is in high demand in your locality. In my case, plantain was in high demand and for that singular reason I made a lot of money trading plantain.

I encourage you, after reading this chapter, to begin contemplating which agro-commodity you can trade and profit from. Delve deep into your thoughts, jot down your ideas, and most importantly, take action. I assure you, there is ample money to be made in this field.

LIFE LESSONS

- Ensure there is a market demand for the agricultural commodity before trading.

- Secure your market before starting to trade by building relationships with potential buyers.

- Market research is crucial to understand customer needs and preferences.

- Consider factors such as production costs, transportation, storage, and quality control.

- Leverage social media to secure and expand your market.

Agribusiness Consulting,
HERE I COME

Chapter Six

"Never underestimate the power of thought; it is
the greatest path to discovery."
— Idowu Koyenikan

After graduating from university in 2019, I
embarked on the one-year journey of the Nigerian
Youth Service Corps (NYSC). At that point, I
held two certificates: one from the university and the other
declaring me a proud business owner.

In 2020, I made up my mind to increase the revenue
my business generated. How was I going to do this?
I immediately set ambitious goals and targets, but
unfortunately, in March of that same year, the unexpected
happened. Covid. The outbreak of the Covid-19 pandemic
brought our operations to a screeching halt. We were forced
to close down temporarily, and I was uncertain of what
the future would look like.

During those months of being confined indoors, my mind raced with thoughts on how to get our business back on its feet. It became clear to me that we needed to pivot our business into something else, something that could weather the storm and offer new opportunities.

Crowdfunding for agriculture was never a path I favoured, especially considering the influx of agricultural crowdfunding platforms that emerged in the wake of Covid-19. I knew deep down that it wasn't a sustainable solution, and true enough, many of those platforms crashed in 2021 with several people losing millions of their hard-earned money in the process. But that's a discussion for another time.

As I pondered over our next move, an idea began to take shape. I realised that I could leverage my vast experience in the agricultural sector and turn it into a profitable venture. After all, I had spent a decade immersed in this industry, acquiring valuable insights and knowledge along the way. It became clear to me that there were people out there willing to pay for my expertise, especially since I had cultivated a personal brand within the agricultural sector. The question that arose next was: how could I transform my experience into a profitable enterprise?

And so, the concept of my consulting company was born. Through this venture, I would be able to monetise my experience, offering it as a service to those seeking guidance and expertise in the agricultural field. I recognised that there was a market for my insights and solutions, and by establishing a consulting company, I could trade my experience for profit. This realization filled me with a renewed sense of purpose and determination to overcome the challenges that lay ahead. Little did I know that this pivot would open up a world of opportunities and pave the way for a new chapter in my entrepreneurial journey.

As I sat down and pondered the direction of our consulting firm, I took the time to articulate the services we would offer to our clients. It was important for us to have a clear understanding of our target audience and how we could effectively reach out to them. Thankfully, through careful consideration and divine guidance, we were able to find answers to these questions, ultimately giving birth to our consulting firm.

Our firm would specialise in various areas, including farm setup, product development, agri-research, and financial development projects, primarily focused on developing countries.

Our clients would consist of business owners, farmers, cooperatives, agrifood manufacturers, and local authorities. Our core focus was to assist individuals and organizations in setting up and managing their farms, while also facilitating the marketing and distribution of their produce. However, our vision extended beyond just working with individual clients.

Looking to the future, we had ambitious plans to collaborate with government agencies, private sector companies, and leading international development organizations. Our aim was to conduct comprehensive market research on key value chains, analyse and shape policies, develop strategies, launch innovative businesses, and build ecosystem solutions. We envisioned organising various convenings and conferences, as well as providing training programs that promote sustainable agricultural development across Africa.

Furthermore, we harbored the intention of establishing a private investment firm specifically focused on the food and agricultural sector in Africa. Our goal was to create an agri-investment and advisory firm that would play a pivotal role in developing world-class farming and integrated agribusinesses across the entire value chain, with a particular emphasis on frontier markets. We were determined to work closely with our clients, offering innovative solutions that address food security, economic growth, and environmental sustainability in challenging environments.

In pursuit of these objectives, we planned to provide a range of key services. These services would encompass investment advisory, financial analysis, risk assessment, project management, market intelligence, and strategic planning. Through our comprehensive approach and unwavering commitment, we aspired to make a significant impact in the agricultural landscape, fostering growth and transformation for the benefit of individuals, communities, and nations.

Specifically, we will work with clients to provide innovative solution to food security, economic and environmental sustainability in challenging environments and will provide some key services such as:

1. Supporting corporate business to establish operations in Africa

2. Identification of investment opportunities for range of investors

3. Assisting businesses to become "investment ready" (expansion capital or outright sale)

4. Acquisition financial and technical due diligence

5. Financing (grant, debt and equity)

6. Non-executive board management

Project management consultancy. We intend to provide consultancy for both the public and private sector since we launched our consulting firm we have consult for some big organization including two privates universities, cooperatives and 53 privates firms belonging to individuals, I would have love to mention these organization for privacy sake I will keep them to myself but if you have been following me on social media you would have seen me posting some of these organization on social media.

They are so many ways you can sell your experience for profit today, mine was through consulting and you could do same but there are other ways such as;

- Coaching programs

- Mentorship program

- Consulting

- Public speaking

- Selling courses

- Books

- Lecturing

Coaching Programs

you can become a coach to others by guiding them through life using your experience and you will earn money from it. There is different type of coach such as life coach or career coach etc. and as a coach you can launch your coaching program for some fees. A coaching program is an offer that you as a coach create to reflect and deliver your original teaching style and materials in an unique way you can do this for a fee.

Mentorship

You can create a proper structure where you mentor people one on one to help improve their performance games and you will charge for it and yes, people will pay for it.

Consulting

You could also decide to run your consulting firm like I do and you will earn from it as well.

Public Speaking

You can decide to go into public speaking where you share your experiences with others and inspire them, motivate them and encourage them with your own past experience, you can also decide to charge for a fee for overtime as you keep building your audience.

Selling Courses

You can decide to teach people how to navigate life using your experience as a framework and guide for them and you can package it as a course and start selling it for a fee, you can make money for this too

Books

You can decide to document your experience as a book either hard copy or e-books and you can make so much money from this. As you can see that is what I did with this book, I document my entire farm experience in this book you can do same and make money from them.

There are many ways you can make money from your experience. I have itemized some ways and I know there are other ways, you can do your research. There is someone out there who is willing to learn from your experience, there is someone who is currently passing through what you have passed through and will be willing to learn how you navigate your way through. Document your experience and start selling it today.

LIFE LESSONS

- In life, one must learn to think strategically. There is always a way out. In the business you are pursuing, if you think strategically, you will find ways to diversify your profile.

- In life, learn to retrospect and reflect. This will help you discover things about yourself. I thank God for COVID; without it, I would not have found my path in consulting yet. The challenging period helped me reflect on my journey, and that reflection gave birth to my consulting firm today.

Networking:

MY SUPERPOWER

_____

Chapter Seven

"Networking is an investment in your business.
It takes time and when done correctly can yield
great results for years to come."
-- Diane Helbig

I **have always been one to easily** connect with people since I was a child. As early as 7 years, I had already begun moving with bigger people, people who were older than me, and people who were doing amazing things in society. Growing up, these people inspired me to go for the best in life irrespective of my age. I was bold and very courageous to approach people irrespective of who they were. This also endeared me to so many people as they saw it as a gift from God- the gift of networking. As a child, many people thought I was going to become a Pastor, so I networked with so many bigger Pastors in my city. As I grew, I took note of this gift, and of course, the power of networking was transforming my life. I began to pay attention to these lessons and ask myself strategic questions at every networking opportunity, such as "What did you say that made the person love you or want you in their space?". Then I would take note of the things I said and practice them more, and over time, these things have transformed my life. Networking is very important for branding and attaining global heights. Networking is not done in the house, the first thing to do is to move in order to network with people. When building a brand, you must look for others in that same industry to network with. Find out the top five people in the industry and strategically position yourself to connect with them.

One of the key places to network with people is at events. It is essential to seek events relevant to your industry and prepare for these events. As an agriculturist, I travel a lot, attending agricultural conferences and moving to and fro various cities. Even as a student, I shuffled a lot of travels until I moved to Lagos, just to attend relevant events and network with people.

HOW TO NETWORK AT AN EVENT

Networking at events can be a great way to expand your professional connections and build valuable relationships.

For me, these are the simple ways I network with people at events:

I ensure I arrive early. This gives me an opportunity to engage with people before the event gets too crowded. It is often easier to strike up conversations with a smaller group of people.

I set clear goals. Before leaving for an event, I define my intention for going and what I want to achieve from the event. Sometimes, it could be to meet a certain individual, learn about certain things about my industry, or even collaborate with other people.

Start with a smile. When you meet someone, start with a smile. A smile is a warm gesture that makes one approachable. Most of the time, I always smile with accompanying eye contact and handshake when approaching others. Although, ethically, it is advised to allow the lady to extend a handshake first.

Have an elevator pitch. Prepare a brief and concise introduction that highlights who you are, what you do, and what makes you unique. These projects a strong first impression to whoever you are networking with.

Listen attentively. Networking is not just about talking. It is equally important to listen to others. Show genuine interest in their own stories and perspectives, and if you must disagree, do so politely.

Ask open-ended questions. Open-ended questions, rather than yes-or-no questions, encourage conversations. For example, these are open-ended questions you could use in a conversation; *"What project are you currently working on?", "How did you get started with this food processing?", "What made you venture into this particular field?"*

Find common ground. Look for shared interests or experiences that can serve as conversation starters, which could be hobbies to mutual connections. Even Jesus Christ used this strategy to start a conversation with the woman at the well. He also understood and implemented networking.

Exchange business cards or contact information. When going to events, it is important to print business cards that contain relevant contact information. These days, there are cards that have codes that people can scan to connect with you. You can also get that if possible. While networking, it is also important to collect the other person's contact information. This will make it easy to follow up after the event.

Use social media. Connect with people you meet on social media platforms, especially LinkedIn. Good positioning on LinkedIn, which includes a good profile, is very essential. There is a certain way you present yourself on LinkedIn so that you are viewed as a professional that others want to connect with. This allows for good nurturing and maintenance of professional relationships online.

Attend workshops and breakout sessions. Participate in discussions and workshops relating to your interests. Ask intelligent questions during these sessions and workshops. This is an excellent way of meeting like-minded individuals and engaging in meaningful conversations. If there is an opportunity to volunteer to be part of the event committee, it is a very good platform to network and build relationships.

Follow up after the event. Reach out to the people you connected with after the event. It is best that you reach out to them in less than 24 hours after connecting with them, expressing your pleasure in connecting with them and suggesting a future meet-up or collaboration. Remember, networking is about building relationships. So you must be genuine, respectful, and approachable. Then you will find that networking becomes an enjoyable and rewarding experience.

HOW TO BUILD STRONGER RELATIONSHIP WITH YOUR NEW NETWORK

After attending events, it is very important to follow up with the contacts and maximise the potential benefits for yourself, your brand, and your business.

These are some strategies I use to follow up with the people I have networked with.

I organise and categorise the contacts I have made. I organise them in such a way that I can follow up on them easily. I categorise their contacts based on their potential value to me and my brand.

I send a personalised message. A personalised message is a key way to show genuine interest and build a strong connection. In my personalised messages, I introduce myself and appreciate the privilege of connecting with them. I also refer to one of our discussions during the event in order to juggle their memories. Then I mention my interest in continuing the conversation or extending further collaborations.

I connect on professional networking platforms. This allows me to expand my professional network and provide platforms for ongoing engagement. Personally, I use LinkedIn, so after the event, I connect with everyone I met on LinkedIn.

Once my request is accepted, I continue with a personalised message.

I provide value or insights. I follow up on communication with them, offering them value in any way I can. I contribute to and support whatever they are doing. I can also introduce them to other professionals who can be of value to them. This demonstrates my willingness to contribute and also helps establish a mutually beneficial relationship. One principle of networking I have learned is to give 90% to the other party and then you can expect 10%. You cannot request anything when you have not given anything to the person. A networker must learn to give. The formula I use for this is EBA- Emotional Bank Account.

I schedule follow-up meetings or calls. If there is a potential for further collaborations or a need for follow-up meetings or calls, I work on it immediately. This allows me to dive deeper into specific topics, explore partnership opportunities, or discuss potential projects. The next time I visit, I will also go with a gift to appreciate them. This helps me to be proactive in suggesting a specific time or proposing a few options to make it easier for our contact to schedule the meeting.

I maintain regular communication. Building relationships requires consistent effort. Stay in touch with your contacts by periodically sharing relevant updates, industry news, or interesting content that aligns with their interests. This puts you on their radar and strengthens the connection over time.

I track and measure interactions and progress with each contact. This allows for easy prioritising of follow-up and monitoring of engagements. This also allows me to keep in touch and measure the effectiveness of networking.

Networking is a long-term investment, and building relationships takes time. Consistency, genuine interest, and providing values, are the key principles to building follow-up activities. By measuring the contacts, you make at events, you increase the likelihood of turning them into valuable connections that can be beneficial to you in the future.

LIFE LESSONS

- Having networking skills can be a gamechanger for you in every aspect of your life. Learn it. Use it.

- When you get into certain places, always keep in mind that there might be someone in that room who will be a connection to the level you desire to be. Don't hold back. Reach out and network correctly.

Chapter Eight

Raising Funds For My
AGRIBUSINESS

Chapter Eight

"To be successful, you have to have your heart in your business, and your business in your heart."
– Thomas Watson, Sr., former CEO, IBM

Funding a business, especially when you're young, can be one of the most challenging aspects of entrepreneurship. In this chapter, I will share how I raised funds for my various agribusiness ventures.

While I had a deep love for agriculture, I knew it required substantial capital investment. So, I sought out another business through which I could raise funds to invest in agriculture. The very first business I started was a boutique, selling both male and female clothing. In a previous chapter, I mentioned how I began this business at my university. Now, I will explain how I raised funds to sustain the shop after acquiring it from the school.

Let me do a little recap: During my first year in university, I accidentally overpaid my school fees by about twenty thousand naira (N20,000). Realising this, I wrote a letter to the school requesting a refund. Fortunately, my request was approved, and I was informed that the excess amount would be deducted from my tuition fees for the following semester. This meant that I would have an extra N20,000 that I could use. I reached out to a friend who owned a boutique at another university to inquire about the cost of opening a boutique at my school. Initially, she suggested that N20,000 would suffice, but later she revised it to N50,000.

Later on; during the holiday break, I joined my family business to raise more money. My mother paid me N10,000, and I saved an additional N30,000. However, when I called my friend again, she increased the amount to N70,000. Determined to reach the target, I sought out other odd jobs and managed to earn an extra N30,000, bringing the total to N80,000. Instead of calling my friend, I reached out to another acquaintance who was traveling to Onitsha. Together, we purchased enough clothes to stock my shop.

This was how I raised the funds for my first business. While I continued selling and making a profit, I also began saving for my agricultural venture. Once I had accumulated a significant portion of the required capital, I approached my dean about utilising the school pond, as I mentioned in a previous chapter. After gaining approval, I needed additional funds for the catfish business. I decided to pitch the idea to my elder brother, who agreed to invest in the business with me. The arrangement was that he would provide the capital and receive a percentage of the business's profits.

Next, I raised funds for my cassava flour (fufu) business. I used part of the profit generated from my catfish venture, and my brother, who was also my investor, contributed additional funds. I processed the cassava from our farm and began supplying shopping malls in Benin, Warri, Asaba, and even some customers in Lagos. As my business needed to scale, I started seeking funds from investors.

The first investor I spoke to was a white woman married to a Nigerian and living in the USA. Impressed by how I managed my catfish business, she offered to invest eighty million naira to set up a factory. However, my very good friend and big brother Rev Soares Oladamola advised me not to accept the funds, citing a lack of sufficient capacity to manage such a large investment.

Similar situations occurred with subsequent investors. Rev Damola consistently advised me to reject their offers. Instead, I opted to pursue grants, as they provided smaller amounts that allowed me to test the waters. Rev Damola was actually the one who taught me how to apply for grants, prepare pitch deck, elevator pitch and even how to effectively develop a business plan.

Winning my first grant

I won my first grant in 2018 from 'Oxfam International in partnership with EdoJobs' on International Youth Day, August 12th. The grant amounted to two hundred thousand naira and included an incubation program. I also received a grant of approximately two hundred and fifty thousand naira from 'Cash your Passion Initiative.'

These grant wins marked the beginning of a series of grants and awards. For example, I was honoured with the Entrepreneur of the Year award, which included one million naira in cash and eight-million-naira worth of advertising from Promedia. Additionally, I made it a personal goal to win at least one grant every month and I actually did. They is an exceeding joy in win grant and it more like a validate to your business idea. It make you believe in your business ideas and build your confident especially as a start-up.

Throughout my journey, I participated in programs such as the Aspiring Entrepreneur Program offered by Fate Foundation and Entreprise Development Centre at Pan Africa University and Lagos Business School. I also engaged with numerous business schools worldwide.

As an entrepreneur, mastering the skill of raising funds for your projects or business ideas is crucial. It is a critical skill that I believe every entrepreneur must learn.

One of the best ways to raise funds for your agribusiness is through grants.

What to consider when applying for a business grant.

In this book I am going to use the Tony Elumelu Empowerment Foundation Grant as a case study as that is one for the biggest grant in Africa.

When applying for a business grant, such as the Tony Elumelu Foundation Grant, there are several important considerations to keep in mind to maximise your chances of success.

The Tony Elumelu Foundation Grant specifically focuses on empowering African entrepreneurs and businesses, so tailoring your application to align with their goals is crucial.

Here are some specific factors to consider:

1. *Eligibility Criteria:* Review the eligibility criteria provided by the Tony Elumelu Foundation thoroughly. Ensure that your business and you as an entrepreneur meet all the specific requirements before proceeding with the application.

2. *Business Plan*: Develop a clear and detailed business plan that outlines your business idea, target market, revenue model, growth strategy, and social and economic impact. The foundation emphasises the importance of a well-defined and viable business plan.

3. *Alignment with Foundation Goals:* Demonstrate how your business aligns with the Tony Elumelu Foundation's mission of empowering African entrepreneurs, creating jobs, and contributing to economic growth and development in Africa.

4. *Innovation and Originality*: Highlight the unique aspects of your business idea or approach. Show how your business stands out and brings innovation to the market.

5. *Social Impact*: Emphasise the social impact your business will create in your community or country. Showcase how your business contributes to solving a specific problem or addresses a pressing need.

6. Sustainability: Prove that your business is financially sustainable in the long term. Present a well-thought-out financial model that shows how you will generate revenue and manage expenses.

7. Past Achievements: If applicable, share any significant achievements, milestones, or recognition your business

has already attained. This can add credibility to your application.

8. Leadership and Team: Highlight the expertise and experience of you and your team. Show that you have the skills and knowledge to execute the business plan effectively.

9. Budget and Fund Allocation: Create a detailed budget for how you will use the grant funds. Clearly outline how the funds will be allocated and how they will contribute to your business's growth and success.

10. Metrics and Evaluation: Clearly define how you will measure the success of your business and the impact of the grant funds. Setting measurable goals and objectives will demonstrate accountability and effectiveness.

11. Recommendations: If possible, include letters of recommendation from relevant industry experts, mentors, or clients. Positive feedback and endorsements can strengthen your application.

12. Professional Presentation: Ensure that your application is well-organised, professionally presented, and free from errors. Review and edit your application thoroughly before submission.

13. Passion and Dedication: Convey your passion and commitment to your business and the positive change

you aim to create in your community. Show that you are dedicated to making a difference.

Remember that the competition for business grants can be fierce, so take the time to carefully prepare your application and demonstrate the value and potential of your business. Be authentic, thoughtful, and strategic in presenting your case to the Tony Elumelu Foundation or any other grant provider.

Few things that must be included in a business plan for presentation to investors.

When creating a business plan for presentation to investors, it's essential to provide a comprehensive and well-structured document that conveys your business's vision, strategy, and potential for growth.

Here are some key elements that must be included in a business plan for investor presentations:

1. *Executive Summary:* Summarise the key points of your business plan concisely. Include your business idea, market opportunity, competitive advantage, financial highlights, and the amount of funding you are seeking.

2. *Company Overview*: Provide an overview of your company, including its history, legal structure, location,

and mission statement. Explain the problem your business addresses and the solution it offers.

3. *Market Analysis:* Present a detailed analysis of your target market, industry trends, and customer needs. Include market size, growth potential, and any relevant data or research to support your claims.

4. *Competitive Analysis: I*dentify your main competitors and analyse their strengths and weaknesses. Clearly explain your competitive advantage and how your business stands out in the market.

5. *Product or Service Description:* Describe your product or service in detail, including its features, benefits, and unique selling points. Highlight how it addresses the needs of your target customers.

6. *Marketing and Sales Strategy:* Outline your marketing and sales plans to reach your target audience effectively. Include details about your promotional activities, pricing strategy, and distribution channels.

7. *Operational Plan:* Provide insights into the day-to-day operations of your business. Explain the production process, supply chain management, and any necessary equipment or technology.

8. *Management Team:* Introduce the key members of your management team and their roles. Highlight their expertise and experience relevant to the business.

9. *Financial Projections:* Include detailed financial forecasts, such as income statements, balance sheets, and cash flow projections. Use realistic assumptions and explain how you arrived at these numbers.

10. *Funding Request and Use of Funds:* Clearly state the amount of funding you are seeking from investors and the type of investment. Specify how the funds will be used to support business growth and development.

11. *Risk Analysis:* Identify potential risks and challenges that your business may face and explain how you plan to mitigate them. Investors appreciate a thorough understanding of the risks involved.

12. *Exit Strategy:* Describe your long-term vision for the business and the potential exit options for investors. This may include a timeline for a possible sale or public offering.

13. *Appendix:* Include any additional information that supports your business plan, such as market research data, product images, customer testimonials, and legal documents.

Remember to keep your business plan well-organised, focused, and visually appealing. Use charts, graphs, and other visuals to make complex information more accessible. Tailor the plan to the specific needs and interests of your target investors, highlighting the aspects that align with their investment criteria and preferences. Practice presenting the business plan confidently and be prepared to answer any questions that investors may have during the presentation.

Few things that must be included in a pitch deck for presentation to investors

A pitch deck is a concise and visually engaging presentation that provides an overview of your business or startup to potential investors.

For me, a pitch deck is a visual engaging presentation of your business plan but more concise and straight to the point as investors do not have so much time to listen to you. Prepare to present your pitch deck in less than 10 to 15 minutes.

While the content may vary depending on your specific business and industry, here are some essential elements that must be included in a pitch deck for a presentation to investors:

1. Introduction: Start with a compelling and memorable introduction that includes the name of your company, logo, and a brief tagline that conveys your value proposition.

2. Problem Statement: Clearly define the problem or pain point that your business addresses. Explain why this problem is significant and how it affects your target market.

3. Solution: Present your product or service as the solution to the identified problem. Describe how your offering is innovative, unique, and better than existing alternatives.

4. Market Opportunity: Provide data and insights about the size of your target market and the growth potential. Investors need to see that there is a substantial opportunity for your business to scale.

5. Business Model: Explain how your business will generate revenue. Describe your pricing strategy, sales channels, and any other sources of income.

6. Traction and Milestones: Highlight any significant achievements your business has reached so far. This could include sales figures, partnerships, key clients, or milestones achieved.

7. Competitive Analysis: Identify your main competitors and explain how your product or service stands out

in comparison. Showcase your competitive advantage and barriers to entry.

8. Go-to-Market Strategy: Describe your marketing and distribution strategy. Explain how you plan to reach your target customers and promote your product or service effectively.

9. Financial Projections: Present your financial forecasts, including revenue projections, expense estimates, and key financial metrics. Be realistic and transparent in your assumptions.

10. Use of Funds: Clearly outline how you intend to use the investment funds you are seeking. Break down the allocation of funds into different categories, such as product development, marketing, or hiring.

11. Team: Introduce the key members of your team, highlighting their expertise, experience, and roles within the company. Investors often invest in the team as much as they do in the idea.

12. Investment Ask: State the amount of funding you are seeking from investors and the type of investment (equity, convertible note, etc.). Be specific about the terms and conditions.

13. Milestones and Exit Strategy: Explain the key milestones you plan to achieve with the investment and your long-

term vision for the business. Include information about the potential exit strategy for investors.

14. Visuals: Use visuals such as charts, graphs, images, and product demonstrations to make the presentation more engaging and easier to understand.

15. Contact Information: Provide your contact details so investors can reach out to you with questions or for follow-up discussions.

Keep in mind that a pitch deck should be concise and focused, usually consisting of 10-20 slides. Practice your pitch to ensure you can confidently present the information in a clear and compelling manner during the investor presentation.

LIFE LESSONS

- Your first funds must come from you: If you read my story, you will notice the first investment into my business came from me. If you cannot invest in your own idea, why should someone else invest?

- Your second pool of funds should come from your family and friends: No investor will believe your idea if your family and friends don't believe in it. You should be able to sell the idea to your family members or a friend, convince them enough to invest in it before you start looking for investors outside.

- The third option should be grants: Grants are funds you don't need to pay back, money gotten from grants can be used to test your business idea if it will work or not.

- Loan is not an option for a start-up and if you must crowdfund, never promise them profit, actually crowdfunding is not for business idea. Non-Government Organizations (NGO) are best suited to use this method to fund their projects. I will advice you to leave crowdfunding if your business is not a social enterprise or Non-Government Organization (NGO).

- Never accept funds from investors if you know you do not have the capacity to manage it. If you reject the funds, they will see you as someone with integrity.

- I also observe a lot of people want to invest in your business but they don't want to be part of it or play any role in the business. They only want return on investment, be careful of such people especially if you don't have the capacity to manage the funds.

Positioning Yourself For
FUNDING

Chapter Nine

"The journey of a thousand miles begins with a
single step."
– Lao Tzu

Positioning your agribusiness for funding is a
crucial step that requires careful planning and
effort. In this chapter, I will guide you through
strategic ways to position your agribusiness for funds.
Pay close attention to these strategies as they can greatly
increase your chances of success.

1. Register your business. Make sure to register
   your business with the appropriate government
   authority in your country. In Nigeria, for
   example, you would register your agribusiness
   with the Corporate Affairs Commission (CAC).
   If possible, try to have co-founders and directors
   on board so that you can register your business
   as a limited company. However, if you are unable

to meet the requirements for a limited company, you can still register it as a company.

2. Build a brand. Focus on building a brand for your business and establishing a strong online presence for yourself. Be visible and vocal online. Building a brand means creating an online presence for your business on various social media platforms such as Facebook, Instagram, Twitter, LinkedIn, WhatsApp Business, and Google My Business. Additionally, invest in a professional website where people can visit and learn more about what your business is all about.

Research has shown that many investors now use digital platforms to learn about what CEOs are saying. Therefore, it is important to generate buzz and create noise on social media. Show up consistently and showcase the proof of concept for your business. Engage with your audience and build traction by constantly talking about your products and services. You can even initiate conversations with investors directly on social media platforms. If you establish yourself as knowledgeable in your field, investors may even reach out to you to discuss investment opportunities. Remember to cultivate healthy relationships with investors and nurture them over time. I have personally connected with numerous investors through social media, especially on LinkedIn.

Consistency is key when it comes to maintaining your online presence. By consistently putting in effort towards branding, you can reach a point where investors recognise you even before you introduce yourself. Keep in mind that the key to success lies in staying consistent and persistent in your branding efforts.

3. Create a business plan. If you must successfully raise funds for your business, you must have a business plan. Having an idea or concept is not enough; that is just the beginning. You must have workable business plan. The scriptures say, "Suppose one of you wants to build a tower. Won't you first sit down and estimate the cost to see if you have enough money to complete it" When you have a business plan investor take you seriously. According to a survey conducted by Small Business Trends, a business plan doubles your chances for success.

Let dive into the numbers to get a proper

understanding of your data: 2,877 people completed the survey, of those number, 995 had completed a business plan:

- 297 of them (36%) secured a loan.

- 280 of them (36%) secured investment capital.

- 499 of them (64%) had grown their business.

- 1556 of the 2,877 had not get completed working on their business plan.

- 222 of them (18%) secured a loan.

- 219 of them (18%) secured investment.

- 501 of them (43%) had grown their business.

You can see from the survey the number of people who secured investment capital and loan was high for those who have business plan than those who those not have any yet.

A business plan doubles your chances of accessing funds for your business. A robust business plan helps potential investors understand your vision, goals and financial projections of your business. You will also understand the risks of your strategy and the impact of any deviation from the plan.

4. Get your pitch Deck Ready. A solid pitch deck is necessary if you 're seeking to raise money for your business. Potential investors are interested in a pitch deck that works well. It starts a conversation with them about your business that ideally results in an investment. The story of your company should be told in your pitch deck.

An investor's initial perception of your company will probably be influenced by your pitch deck and presentation. Your object is to stimulate potential investors' interest in your company because they rarely invest after only one meeting.

A pitch deck is a detailed but concise snapshot of your company to attract investors. Understanding the necessary elements of a successful pitch deck can help bring you one step closer to the funding you need.

Your pitch deck should contain a summary of what the business is about, the problem you are trying to solve, your target market, the solution to the problem the business is solving, market and sales strategy, your traction/milestones, your competitors, your team members, your business financials and the amount /fund you want. Your pitch deck should not be more than 10 slides and if you can reduce it further more it will be better.

Few more things you should take note of in preparing a pitch deck:

- Your pitch deck must be straightforward, don't overload investor with information

- Clearly explained your ideas detailed in bullet point

- Make your pitch deck very attractive

- Master the art of storytelling, this skill will help you present your pitch properly. it will help your pitch to be capitative and investor will find you relatable.

5. Master your numbers. Understand your numbers, I mean understand the business finance, understand the number of sales to break even, know your profit and under stand the return of investment. Have a clear-cut understanding of how much funds you need and what you want to do with the funds. You must master your

numbers.

6. Have a business record. Have a business record probably in a book or accounting software's. One of the ways you can communicate to investors about your business is through record keeping.

   Record keeping help you know your numbers. Recording keeping give you room to pitch your business to investors.

   When you have your records right, make statement like;

   · Consistently, there has been a 10-15% increase in our sales

   · From xyz brand we have 75% of our major sales

   · Between the month of January to June, we have ben able to cut our admin expense by 5%

   · If you invest in us, we assure you of a 10% return of investment.

   Imagine you speak like this to investors; you will be taken very seriously.

   Before you start raising money for your business you need to be sure that your business is investment ready?

You need to ask yourself this following question:

1. Have you built the right products/ services?

2. How well have you bootstrapped the business?

3. How well does your business match investors objectives?

4. What are investors objectives?

Before you start raising funds for your business you need to understand what investors objectives.

The following are investors objectives

1. The social impact of the business: What is the social impact of the business?

2. Local jobs creations: What local jobs is the business creating or will be creating?

3. The return on investment: What is the return on investment?

4. Environmental impact: What is the environmental impact of the business?

5. Technology driven: Is the business technology driven?

6. Inclusion: What inclusion strategy are you building into the organization?

This and many more are some of the investor's objectives.

Sources of funds for your agribusinesses

1. Families/friends

2. Angel investors

3. Competitions, prizes and awards

4. Accelerators programs

5. Incubation programs

6. Grants

7. Crowdfunding

8. Venture capital

9. Challenges funds

10. Fellowships

11. Impact investors

12. Private's equity investors

13. Loans

14. Trade credit

15. Payment advance

16. Initial public offer

17. DFI

18. Corporate investor

A FEW MORE THINGS YOU SHOULD TAKE NOTE OF

1. *Establishing a strong track record is crucial for securing funding for an agribusiness.* A strong track record includes a history of profitable operations, positive cash flow, and a reputation for delivering quality products or services. This demonstrates to potential investors or lenders that the business is financially stable and has a track record of success.

2. *Building a diverse portfolio* can help reduce risk and increase the likelihood of success for an agribusiness. This can include diversifying products or services,

crop diversification, or a combination of traditional and innovative farming methods. Diversifying operations can help mitigate the impact of market fluctuations and increase the chances of success for the business.

3. *Networking and building relationships* is an important step in securing funding for an agribusiness. Building relationships with potential investors or lenders can help increase the visibility of the business and increase the likelihood of funding. Attend industry events, join trade associations, and connect with other agribusiness professionals to expand your network.

4. *Showing how your business will make a positive impact* on the community and the environment is an important factor for securing funding. Investors and lenders are increasingly interested in funding businesses that have a positive impact on society. Be prepared to demonstrate how your agribusiness will contribute to sustainable food production, conservation of natural resources, and economic development.

5. *Having accurate, up-to-date, and easily accessible financial records* is crucial for securing funding for an agribusiness. This includes financial statements,

tax returns, and cash flow projections. This will help potential investors or lenders to evaluate the financial health of the business and help determine whether it is a viable investment.

6. *Government provides various schemes and subsidies for the agribusiness sector.* Identifying the schemes and subsidies that apply to your agribusiness, and using them to help secure funding.

7. *Be prepared to give up a portion of your equity in exchange for funding.* This may include giving up a percentage of ownership in your agribusiness or issuing shares to investors.

8. *Incorporating technology* in your agribusiness can help increase efficiency and productivity. This can include precision agriculture, automation, and data analytics. Demonstrating that your agribusiness is using the latest technology can help make it more attractive to potential investors or lenders.

9. *Look for a SDGs sustainable goal that is tailored to your business.* Your business should be solving one or two SDGs goals. Study the SDGs goal and look for the one your business idea in line with. Your business must be offering a solution to some of the SDGs goal.

10. Securing funding can be a long and difficult process. Be prepared to face rejection and keep trying. Keep your business plan and financials up to date, and be ready to adapt to changing market conditions. It is important to be persistent and to continue to pursue funding opportunities.

LIFE LESSONS

- In the game of life, you must learn to be resilient because fundraising, rejection is common in the funding process. Learning to handle rejection with resilience and perseverance is crucial for both personal and proefessional growth.

- You must master how to communicate your business idea effectively to potential investors, which requires clarity, persuasion, and confidence. These skills are transferable to various aspects of life, including personal relationships and career advancement.

Chapter Ten

How To Navigate
TOUGH SEASONS

Chapter Ten

"If you always attach positive emotions to the things you want, and never attach negative emotions to the things you don't, then that which you desire most will invariably come your way."
– Matt D. Miller

I HAVE BEEN ASKED SEVERAL TIMES WHAT THE TOUGHEST moment in business is for me. The agricultural business has its own challenges, and I have had my share; fire burn experiences, a few losses in investments in the agricultural business space, and a lot more. Let me share one of the experiences that stood out for me. When my wife was still my fiancé, she used to go to the farm with me along with my younger brother. I was still in school at this time, and I wrote to one of my uncles about my need for land and requested one of his plots of land to farm. I planned on planting vegetables like cucumber, watermelon, and some other short-term crops, to make money and then invest in my business. I had heard that the quickest way to make cash from the agricultural business was to invest in short-term crops. So, I started out by clearing the land to prepare it for farming.

After clearing, my fiancé who is now my wife, my younger brother and I started to plant watermelons and treated seeds of maize, which was quite a tiring endeavour. It took us about 4-5 days to plant on two plots of land but at last, we planted.

After planting, we were willing to maintain it as we were determined to see it grow. Then, my manager who was managing my farm reached out to me to help maintain this one too, After much contemplation, I agreed since it was not so far from the other farm he was managing.

One day, I got to the farm only to discover that weeds had taken over the farm. In farming, maintaining the crop after planting is very important; the more the farmland is maintained, the more the crop that has been planted will do well. Otherwise, weeds will take over and over time, the weeds will kill the crops. Although, whenever I called the young man to ask about the farm, he always assured me the crops were doing well and he was maintaining the land accordingly. As a result of this, the crops did not do well, especially the watermelon. This was a very frustrating and painful experience for me, it made my wife so angry and completely threw us off balance. We lost the crops and also the efforts that went into that farmland at that time.

Pondering how to handle the situation, I spoke to my pastors, Rev Oladamola Soares, who advised me to let go of the young man and find someone else to manage the farmlands. This experience reflected my weakness in managing people, especially my workers, so I had to step up in that area as a leader. This pushed me to not just learn how to farm but also manage and lead people. One of the ways I overcame this tough situation was by visiting other farms.

There were times I would visit farms in Benin City with one of my lecturers, Dr Tony. While visiting, I would ask questions about management and pay attention to their techniques and principles. I also realised that I learned principles of farming in school but I was not taught how to manage people, which I think is essential for the curriculum of agriculture students.

Of course, I also had to read books on leadership and management. The drive for knowledge helped me in these challenges. Farm workers are one of the hardest people to manage because most of them are uneducated and communication is difficult. Hence, special skills are required to manage these people. After this experience, I visited a lot of farmlands, including an excursion as a student to Nile 4 and Presco; even during my internship days at Songa Delta, whenever I had the opportunity to be at one of these farmlands, my focus was their management skills and leadership. I took time to study the systems and structures of these farms that enhanced effective management. For instance, one of the structures Songa Delta put in place was taking in students for internship programs.

Let me capture one of the events that transformed my life. After I finished at Benson Idahosa University, I proceeded to my NYSC and was posted to Jigawa. After my three weeks in Jigawa, I redeployed to Lagos. The major reasons for my redeployment were to network with people and attend relevant events in my industry. As a student, I often travelled from Benin to Lagos to attend events. I understood the power of networking and events in my industry, so I saved money to make these trips.

Sometimes, I arrive in Lagos late at night to attend an event on Saturday morning. At other times, I left Lagos late and arrived in Benin City so late that I had to spend the night at the park. There was one event that stood out for me during my service year in Lagos at the Federal Institute of Industrial Research, Oshodi.

I attended the event, Lagos Farmers Convention hosted by Varden Farms and Resort at Epe. I was not aware of the distance where the event was to take place, I was just so interested in learning so much about farming as I realised it was an event that could change my life. I registered for the event and embarked on the journey on the due date. It was a funny experience for me. I prepared N2000 for the transportation not knowing that the amount could not even get me to Epe.

While driving to the destination, I met someone who was also going for the event and agreed to cover my remaining transportation to the venue until I could withdraw to refund back. At the event, I connected with a lot of people who became part of my journey. The main aim of attending this event was to network with people especially the CEO of Vardens Farm and Resort, Mr Lanre Howells. I got right into it and somehow missed the person who I was to go back with. I finished at the event at about 6pm when everyone had gone home already. I had no money to go home, but I decided to take a bike to a nearby junction. On getting to the junction, someone offered to pay the bike money. I did not have my NYSC card with me but I just entered the buses and explained that I did not have money. The driver warned me not to try it again as Lagos was not a safe place for that kind of act. On getting to Lekki, a woman going to Ibadan gave me some cash which eventually took me home. My determination to network and connect with people in my industry fueled this experience.

I kept in touch with Mr Lanre Howells, The CEO of Varden Farms and Resort, and I nurtured the relationship. Towards the end of my NYSC, I reached out to him as a result of my quest for knowledge to learn more about fresh vegetables and fruits, as that was what we were dealing with. Two months before my passing out, he obliged to make space for me on his farm as they were setting up a new farm at Owode. I got this job even though many people applied because the CEO facilitated my application.

I became a top manager at this farm, connected with many people, and learned a lot about systems and structuring and building systems for businesses. I got to manage people from across different parts of the country. It was indeed an exciting experience. Vardens also had a consulting firm which gave me the opportunity to learn a few consulting tips. After a while, I resigned from Varden Farms to start my own consulting Firm. I combined the knowledge I had gained from Varden farm and Songa

Delta to build my firm. I consulted for various firms and also helped several people to start up their farms and other businesses.

This is how far the drive for knowledge and the power of networking took me. Working at Vardens was a pleasant experience for me and the management team was great. They were a great part of my journey. Today, I have been able to consult for about 35-45 farms and set up over 62 farms. My story emphasises the importance of attending events and networking with people. Lagos Farmers Convention inspired the Africa's Farmers Convention that I host today where I gather Farmers from all over Africa to come speak about agriculture in Africa. Mr Lanre Howells was not just my boss, he was also my role model at that particular time of my life.

The knowledge I gained did not go to waste at all- during my internship at Songa Delta, my excursions at school, my visiting different farms and my work at Varden Farms. After my marriage the plan to go study outside the country came while still running the consulting. Consulting was not a very frequent job so I needed a consistent source of income to take care of my home and raise money to support my travel journey so I started looking for jobs while doing my consulting job by the side in order to fulfill my dreams.

In January 2022, I applied for so many jobs and finally got an interview with TL Farms which landed me the job. I resumed with TL Farms on the 1st of March. All these experiences I had gathered working with different organizations helped me while working with TL Farms. TL Farms was into oil processing, oil farming, banga. They had about 98 hectares of land at the time we were building the processing unit. I came in and put all my experiences to use which helped skyrocket their sales from about 2 drums to 8 drums, and manage leadership more effectively. The knowledge you gather, experiences you go through, skill you acquire, no matter the stage you are at, will be helpful as you journey in life. No knowledge is a waste and no opportunity to learn should be taken for granted.

LIFE LESSONS

- Learning is a constant. As the saying goees, the day you stop learning, you die. You must keep learning to be able to reinvent yourself.

- Put your dream in front of you. Keep chasing your dream.

Building a Sought-After

BRAND

Chapter Eleven

A brand is a voice and a product is a souvenir.
- Lisa Gansky

In the last few years, I have built a strong brand in the Agricultural industry and I am still growing my brand. So, in this chapter I am going to sharing with you how you can build a strong brand for yourself in the agricultural industry.

Before we move on let's look at what is branding.

What is branding?

I am so sure if some of you hear the name Kenneth Obayuwana, the picture of a farm boy or an agricultural enthusiasm will come to your mind, that is what we call branding. It is the ability to create strong impressions in the heart of people even when you are not in the room.

Branding is what people say or think about you when you are not in the room.

Branding is the process of creating a unique name, design, symbol, and/or message that identifies and distinguishes a company, product, or service from its competitors in the marketplace. It involves the creation of a consistent image and reputation that resonates with customers and helps to build trust and loyalty over time.

Brand is what people say when you are not in the room. Brand is who you are and what people think and feel about you.

Effective branding requires a deep understanding of the target audience and their needs, as well as a clear and compelling value proposition that sets the company or product apart from the competition. It also involves developing a brand identity that is consistent across all touchpoints, from the company website and social media profiles to packaging, advertising, and customer service.

Ultimately, successful branding is about creating a strong emotional connection with customers that goes beyond the functional benefits of the product or service, and helps to build long-term relationships based on trust, loyalty, and shared values.

What personal branding?

Personal branding is the process of creating a unique and memorable image or reputation for oneself, with the aim of distinguishing oneself from others in a professional or social context. It involves developing a clear and consistent message that communicates one's values, expertise, and unique qualities, and aligns with one's personal and professional goals.

In the age of social media and online networking, personal branding has become increasingly important for individuals seeking to establish themselves as thought leaders, entrepreneurs, or experts in their field. A strong personal brand can help to increase visibility, attract new opportunities and clients, and establish credibility and authority.

To develop a personal brand, one should start by defining their personal mission statement, values, and unique selling proposition. This involves identifying one's strengths, passions, and areas of expertise, and aligning these with the needs and expectations of one's target audience.

Personal branding also involves creating a consistent image and message across all channels, from social media profiles and personal websites to business cards and professional attire. This includes choosing a colour scheme, font, and design elements that are reflective of one's personal brand, and using these consistently across all communication channels.

Ultimately, successful personal branding is about establishing oneself as an authentic and trustworthy authority in one's field, and building a strong network of like-minded individuals who share one's values and vision.

What is a business branding?

A business brand is the identity and image that a company or organization creates and promotes to distinguish itself from its competitors in the marketplace. It encompasses all the elements that make up a company's visual, verbal, and emotional identity, including its name, logo, tagline, messaging, values, and customer experience.

A strong business brand is essential for establishing a company's reputation, building trust with customers, and differentiating it from competitors. It helps to create a distinct and memorable image in the minds of customers, and it can be a powerful tool for driving sales, building loyalty, and attracting new customers.

To create a strong business brand, companies must first

identify their unique selling proposition and target audience, and develop a clear and compelling message that resonates with customers. This involves creating a consistent visual and verbal identity, and ensuring that all brand elements are aligned with the company's mission, values, and goals.

A successful business brand also requires ongoing monitoring and management to ensure that it remains relevant and responsive to changing customer needs and market trends. This includes measuring brand performance, collecting customer feedback, and adjusting brand elements as needed to maintain a strong and positive reputation in the marketplace.

How to build a successful business brand

Building a successful business brand requires a strategic and comprehensive approach that includes the following steps:

1. *Define your brand identity:* This involves developing a clear understanding of your company's mission, values, and unique selling proposition. Identify your target audience and their needs, preferences, and behaviours.

2. *Develop your visual identity:* This includes creating a logo, choosing a color palette, and selecting fonts and design elements that reflect your brand's personality and values.

3. *Create your messaging strategy:* Develop a consistent voice and tone for your brand, and create messaging that aligns with your brand identity and resonates with your target audience.

4. *Build your online presence:* Establish a website and social media profiles that reflect your brand identity and messaging, and engage with your audience through relevant and meaningful content.

5. *Provide a superior customer experience:* Ensure that every interaction with your customers reflects your brand identity and values, and deliver a high-quality product or service that meets or exceeds their expectations.

6. *Consistently deliver on your brand promise:* Maintain a consistent and authentic brand identity across all touchpoints, and deliver on the promises you make to your customers.

7. *Monitor and measure your brand performance:* Regularly assess your brand's performance and

collect feedback from customers, and adjust your brand strategy as needed to maintain a strong and positive reputation in the marketplace.

By following these steps, you can build a successful business brand that resonates with your target audience, sets you apart from your competitors, and drives long-term success for your company.

Different between a personal brand and a business brand

The main difference between personal branding and business branding is that personal branding focuses on creating a reputation and image for an individual, while business branding focuses on creating a reputation and image for a company or organization.

Personal branding is all about establishing a unique and memorable image or reputation for oneself, with the aim of distinguishing oneself from others in a professional or social context. It involves developing a clear and consistent message that communicates one's values, expertise, and unique qualities, and aligns with one's personal and professional goals.

On the other hand, business branding is about establishing a unique and memorable identity for a company or organization, with the aim of distinguishing it from its competitors in the marketplace. It encompasses all the elements that make up a company's visual, verbal, and emotional identity, including its name, logo, tagline, messaging, values, and customer experience.

Another key difference between personal branding and business branding is the level of control that an individual or company has over their brand. Personal branding is largely driven by the individual themselves, and is based on their personality, expertise, and reputation. In contrast, business branding is typically managed by a team of professionals who work to establish and promote the company's brand identity across all touchpoints.

Ultimately, both personal branding and business branding are essential for establishing a strong reputation and identity in the marketplace. While personal branding focuses on the individual, business branding focuses on the organization, and both can be used to build trust, establish credibility, and drive success in today's competitive business environment. Branding is the process of creating a unique name, design, symbol, and/or message that identifies and distinguishes a company, product, or service from its competitors in the marketplace. It involves the creation of a consistent image and reputation that resonates with customers and helps to build trust and loyalty over time.

Effective branding requires a deep understanding of the target audience and their needs, as well as a clear and compelling value proposition that sets the company or product apart from the competition. It also involves developing a brand identity that is consistent across all touchpoints, from the company website and social media profiles to packaging, advertising, and customer service.

Ultimately, successful branding is about creating a strong emotional connection with customers that goes beyond the functional benefits of the product or service, and helps to build long-term relationships based on trust, loyalty, and shared values.

LIFE LESSONS

- You must learn to differentiate yourself in a busy world, and to do that, you need to build a brand.

- As you progress in life, you must take your personal branding seriously. This is what sets you apart in the marketplace of life.

Chapter Twelve

HOW I CHANGED MY LIFE

Chapter Twelve

"The people who are crazy enough to think they
can change the world are the ones who do."
- Steve Jobs

In 2020 I came to realise that at every moment in our lives we have the capacity to change our lives by just making a decision. This realization made me to make a lot of decision that altered my entire life.

First, I decided that I didn't want to be just another farmer, I want to be a big deal in the world of farming known globally. I remember what Tony Robbins said "your life changes the moment you make a new, congruent and committed decision", and that is what exactly happened to me. I also thought about what Herbert A. Simon said "the decision we make lead to real life experience it's one thing to decide to climb a mountain; it's another to actually do it; I have learnt a lot from my experiences.

Experiences are tangible, a lot of people have made life decision that could have change their life but they did not act on their decision, and so they are still in one spot in life. I made a decision and I acted on it and that changed my life forever.

In 2021, I made a decision to study in the UK, I didn't have the money for tuition fees, but I got accepted and started a GoFundMe campaign to raise the money, many people laughed at me and said negative things about me, but I ignored them and stayed focused. I ended up raising the money, that same year, I got some amazing global opportunities.

In my next book title "Harvesting Opportunities" I'll share more about how I got those opportunities. I became an ambassador for NextGen Agriculture Impact Network (NGIN) I got the opportunity to work with young people who have interesting agricultural sector from different countries and even had the opportunity to travel to Costa Rica for a conference and Rome Italy for the World Food Forum Flagship program. Same year, I volunteer for World Food Forum, this was in 2022.

In 2023, I became the first national director, International Association of Agricultural Student and other Related Science (IAAS) UK chapter. An organization with presence in 56+ countries with membership strength of 20,000 students. I spread the organisation across the UK universities and the organization open me to a lot of global opportunities.

I had an opportunity to speak in Global Tech Summit in Paris, France and my research paper got publish in a journal. I got featured in an India magazine, got invited to speak in the 4th Urban Agri World 2023, in Durban, South Africa. I got featured in BBC twice, I got invited to speak in India.

I also co-organised and moderate the World Water Week 2023, the youth session in Stockholm, Sweden. I had great time connecting and networking with several people at the event.

I got invited to speak at two side events in World Food Forum Flagship program 2023, Rome, Italy and also to speak at one of the side events of the committee of World Food Security plenary session 51 in Rome, Italy. I also got the opportunity to attend the high-level dinner with several government officials from different countries and some FAO members during the CFS51, same year, I got invited to speak at the African conference on Agricultural Technologies in Kenya, a conference where the former president Goodluck Ebele Jonathan was speaking as one of the keynote speakers.

Beside all these I have mentioned I had some speaking engagement that was turned down from Canada and US because they were conflicting with my other engagement, but the question is how do a peasant farmer build himself to attract all these global speaking engagement from different country?

Beside speaking engagement, I became the head of the Food Security Think Tank at the Food and Agriculture Youth Institute and that gave me the opportunity to sit on the Food and Agriculture Youth Institute (FAYI) at the time of writing this I currently sit on three board and they are follow; Fayi Board, IAAS Quality Board, NGIN Board.

Yes I currently sit on NGIN Board an organization I was once an ambassador to. Besides sitting on the board of organisations and speaking engagements, I also host the famous "Agritech Founders Diary" on YouTube and podcast. A show where I interview Agritech entrepreneurs and senior operators for 40 minutes they got to share their experience, challenges faced and provide insight into the product and business they are building.

I also launched "Agritech Digest" a media company that focuses on Agritech related news. In our first three months of launching, we had over 5000 people visiting our site and for year 2024 we have two big companies ready to partner and work with us to launch our Journalism School called Agritech Digest Academy, A school set out side to train people on report writing, editing, how to conduct interviews and carry out quality research work in the media space. We hope to host massive event in the Agricultural space in 2024.

In addition, I restructure and rebrand our Agricelerate Global consulting firm, we currently now operate with our office in Nigeria and in the UK. We are fully registered with Nigeria government and the UK government and we hope to start operating in the US in 2024.

Agricelerate Global consulting offering consulting services to agribusinesses looking to expand their operations internationally and locally. We are into Merger and Acquisition of farms and Agribusiness.

All these things happened because of the decision I made, if I had not made that decision to take my life to another level. If I had not made that decision to go study outside Nigeria. If I had not made that decision to run a GoFundMe campaign, maybe I would have still been on one spot.

I had all the excuses like; no money to fund my tuition

fees, no money to study abroad, no uncle or aunty to help me fulfill my dream.

I made a decision to ignore all my excuses and decide to face life and conquer it. I made a decision not to allow my story end in failure, I made a decision not to end in shame and I took action steps on all my decision, if you decide to change your life, all you need to do is to make a decision and take the responsibility on the choices you make. We are all in the spot we are in life today because of one decision we took or we refused to take. You can make a huge progress in life in one year if you decide to take responsibility and act on your decision to progress in the right direction.

In my next book title "Harvesting Opportunities" I will break down how I attract global platforms, ensure you get the book.

LIFE LESSONS

- *The Power of Decisions:* The decisions we make are incredibly powerful. A single decision to change one's path can lead to transformative experience.

- *Persistence and Resilience:* It is very important to stay persistent and resilience in the face of challenges and naysayers. Even when others doubt you, stay focused on your goals and that can lead you to success.

- *Self-Development/Self Improvement:* Self-development/self-improvement can open doors to new opportunities. Go the extra miles to secure quality education, even when facing financial obstacles can be a life changing decision.

- *Believe in Yourself:* Believing in yourself and your ability to make meaningful changes is a fundamental lesson. Your choices can shape your destiny and self-belief is a crucial factor.

CHARITY

Chapter Thirteen

"Happiness doesn't result from what we get, but
from what we give.
- Ben Carson

I 'm fully aware that my life has been as a source of inspiration for a lot of people. Many youths have stumbled on my brand on social media and have been inspired by the life I've led.

I take immense pride in the work I do as a farmer, driven by my passion to use agriculture as a means to combat hunger, create wealth and employment opportunities, and foster equitable economic growth in Africa. My ultimate goal is to uplift millions of people out of poverty. This commitment has been the focal point of my life in recent years.

I firmly believe that life is akin to a credit that must be repaid through impactful contributions. The debt I must settle in life is the positive impact I make on society.

It was this understanding that gave birth to the vision of the "Africa Chambers of Smallholder Farmers." While I have other initiatives through which I give back to society, including "Positive Impact Africa" and the "Africa Start-up Forum," I want to focus on my agricultural journey in this book. Hence, in this chapter, I will concentrate on the impact I've had in the agricultural sector through my NGO called the "Africa Chambers of Smallholder Farmers" and the "Africa Farmers Network."

The "Africa Chambers of Smallholder Farmers" is an initiative aimed at assisting smallholder farmers with technical knowledge through extension agents, conferences, and other forms of support. We provide them with quality seeds for planting, irrigation systems, and financial assistance for their production. The entire purpose of the "Africa Chambers of Smallholder Farmers" is to create a platform that supports and uplifts smallholder farmers. Over the past three years, we have consistently organised the largest gathering of smallholder farmers, known as the "Africa Farmers Convention," where we bring them together and expose them to the latest agricultural trends and ways to improve their farming businesses.

The "Africa Farmers Network" serves as a community for farmers and agricultural students. It was established to foster connections between farmers and the market, creating a platform for mutual support. For students, we have the "Africa Farmers Network of Students," where we aim to expose them to global agricultural opportunities. We provide training on accessing these opportunities and facilitate connections worldwide. Our goal is to enable students to contribute to global agricultural issues. These initiatives are just a few of the platforms I've built over the years to give back to society, and I firmly believe that there are more to come, further supporting the agricultural industry,

It is our collective duty to leave the world in a better state than how we found it. Each and every one of us has the power to make a positive impact on the industry we are a part of. When we contemplate how we can give back to society, we can begin to transform our communities and ultimately the world. While this book primarily focuses on the NGOs I have run in the agricultural industry, it is essential to recognise that I have been involved in other initiatives aimed at making a difference in different areas.

Constantly pondering how we can enhance our society is crucial. It is our responsibility to take action and actively work towards making our communities better. This duty should be ingrained in our minds and hearts, driving us to contribute meaningfully to the betterment of society.

The concept of leaving the world in a better state than we found it holds tremendous significance. It emphasises that our lives should not be spent passively; rather, we should actively seek ways to create positive change. By contributing to our respective industries, we can fulfill this responsibility and make a lasting impact. Whether it involves pioneering new ideas, advocating for necessary changes, or raising the bar for standards and practices, our efforts can propel our industries forward.

The rewards of contributing to our industries extend beyond personal fulfillment. They include a sense of purpose and meaning in our work, the acquisition of valuable skills, the recognition and respect of our peers, and even new opportunities for growth and advancement in our careers.

Yet, the benefits are not limited to the individual. By striving to improve our industries, we are driving progress and positively shaping society. Through advancements in healthcare, advancements in education, and breakthroughs in technology, our contributions ripple outward and touch the lives of countless individuals. When we unite in our efforts to elevate our industries, we create a world that is better equipped to meet the needs and aspirations of all.

In conclusion, it is our shared duty to contribute our best to the improvement of the industry we find ourselves in. By doing so, we not only enhance our own lives and careers but also play an active role in building a better world for everyone. Let us embrace this responsibility and strive to leave a lasting legacy of positive change and progress.

LIFE LESSONS

- We all have a responsibility to contribute to society: Each of us has the power to make a positive impact in the world. It is important to recognise our duty to contribute to society and actively seek ways to make a difference.

- Leaving the world better than we found it is a powerful concept: The idea of leaving a positive impact on the world is a powerful and meaningful one. It reminds us that our actions and contributions can shape a better future for generations to come.

- Contributing to your industry brings personal fulfillment: Actively contributing to your industry, whether through new ideas, advocacy, or advancements, can bring a sense of purpose and fulfillment in your work. It allows you to make a meaningful difference and create a positive impact.

- Collaboration and collective effort drive progress: When we work together to improve our industries and communities, we can achieve greater progress. Collaboration, sharing ideas, and supporting one another's initiatives can lead to significant positive change.

- Making a difference benefit both individuals and society: Contributing to your industry not only benefits your personal growth and career, but it also has a broader impact on society. By advancing industries and sectors, we can address societal needs, create opportunities, and ultimately improve the lives of others.

Chapter Fourteen

WHAT NEXT?

Chapter Fourteen

"The journey of a thousand miles begins with a
single step."
– Lao Tzu

After reflecting on my past achievements, I found myself pondering the next significant step in my journey within the agriculture sector. This question of "What's next?" has been a driving force, and I encourage you to ask it of yourself as well. It's crucial to answer this question and map out your responses as actionable steps.

My next big move is to visualise and execute the grand plan for my life. This 10-year vision that I'm about to outline is the blueprint for the impact I intend to make in the world. I'm sharing it here so that anyone who reads this and shares the desire to collaborate or partner with me in realising this vision can easily connect.

10-Year Vision:

Over the coming decade, I aim to set an inspiring example, proving the incredible influence of individual choices. Here's the vision I have for the next 10 years:

1. Global Agricultural Influence: I'm committed to further solidifying my position as a global agricultural force. My recognition won't solely be for innovative farming practices but also for my dedication to sustainable agriculture.

2. Educational Advancements: I see myself as a lifelong learner, pursuing advanced degrees and specialised knowledge. This pursuit will not only enhance my personal growth but also enable me to contribute significantly to the field of agriculture. Enrolling in MBA programs at prestigious institutions like Harvard and Yale is on the horizon. Fellowship programs will continue to be a part of my journey, enriching my capacity.

3. Author and Mentor: Alongside my continued education, I plan to author more books in the agricultural sector. Sharing experiences, insights, and lessons learned will remain a priority. As my knowledge grows, I aspire to mentor and guide others in their quests for personal, professional, and agricultural growth. My mission is to raise new leaders in the agricultural sector.

4. Philanthropic Endeavours: With the success I've achieved, I envision launching philanthropic initiatives. These efforts will be dedicated to supporting education, sustainable farming practices, rural development, and enhanced agricultural innovations.

5. Prominent Global Speaker: As my expertise grows, I plan to become a sought-after speaker at global conferences. My aim is to inspire individuals worldwide to make impactful decisions and foster positive changes in their lives.

6. Innovation and Technology: I will remain at the forefront of integrating innovative technologies into agriculture. Pioneering new methods that enhance yields, reduce environmental impact, and improve food security will be a focus.

7. International Collaborations: My vision includes establishing meaningful collaborations with agricultural organizations, governments, and NGOs globally. Together, we will work toward addressing the pressing challenges in global food security.

8. Advocacy for Sustainable Practices: As a vocal advocate, I will actively shape policies and practices that prioritises the long-term health of our planet and its inhabitants. Sustainable agriculture will be at the core of this advocacy.

9. Environmental Stewardship: My unwavering commitment to environmental conservation will lead to active involvement in initiatives that protect our ecosystems and biodiversity.

10. Personal Fulfilment and Balance: In this ambitious journey, I will ensure personal well-being and work-life balance, allowing my success in agriculture to be complemented by a happy and fulfilling life.

11. Agritourism Centre: I dream of living on a substantial farm with my family. This Agritourism centre will not only be our home but also an attraction for many, providing educational and recreational opportunities.

12. Leadership Development: I aspire to raise 10,000 young leaders who, in turn, will empower others and contribute to the growth of the agricultural sector.

13. Agricelerate Global Consulting: I hope to expand my consulting firm, Agricelerate Global Consulting, and collaborate with more agribusiness companies to expand their operations.

14. Agritech Digest: My aim is to grow Agritech Digest into the leading agritech media company in the world.

15. Agritech Founders Diary: I aspire to inspire and support over 10,000 agritech founders through Agritech

Founders Diary and various events we will organise.

16. Social Media Influence: I hope to inspire and empower more young people with my work and writings on social media platforms, encouraging them to make impactful decisions and embrace the transformative power of choices.

By following this 10-year vision, I aim to leave an enduring legacy in the world of agriculture, uplift communities, and inspire countless individuals to recognise the transformative power of their own decisions. This vision is not just about shaping my life but also about making a positive impact on our planet and future generations.

LIFE LESSONS

- One of the lessons from this chapter is the need to have the big picture and take one step at a time. keep your ultimate goal in view as you navigate the smaller steps that lead you there. I applied this principle when launching my consulting firm and going through the process of registering it with both the Nigerian and UK governments.

- At the same time, I found myself delving into the world of venture capital and investment, learning the ropes as I went along, I had aspirations of launching my own show called "Agritech Founders Diary" and was in the process of figuring out how to run an entire media company. Instead of waiting until I had all the answers, I chose to take baby steps and learn as I progressed. My advice to others is not to wait until you have everything figured out before taking action. Embrace the concept of baby steps, continuously moving forward while learning and adapting along the way.

- Always be around the business/industry you play in. Learn to always be around that industry you want to do your business. Being around that industry means starting your own little business in that industry or opting to serve at the table of anyone in that industry even if it's to serve them water. What matters is that you are learning.
- Finally, always remember my mantra "Start with the small things, control what you can."

It been a nice ride sharing my stories and experience with you.

Do well to keep in touch with me and share with me what part of my story resonate with you.

About the author

Kenneth Obayuwana is a visionary thinker, globally recognised thought leader, and adept business strategist. As a Certified Management Consultant, he shares practical insights that empower individuals to achieve their utmost potential.

His fervor lies in harnessing agriculture as a force to combat hunger, foster economic prosperity, and drive equitable growth throughout Africa, ultimately lifting millions out of poverty. Kenneth is dedicated to stimulating the mental awakening and values reorientation of young minds.

Kenneth serves as the Managing Director of Agricelerate Global Consulting, a consulting firm committed to assisting agribusinesses in expanding their global operations. He also spearheads Agritech Digest, a prominent media company dedicated to offering profound coverage of the latest agricultural technology trends and innovations. Through this platform, he equips farmers and industry professionals with valuable knowledge and resources.

Additionally, Kenneth hosts "Agritech Founders Diary," a show that features successful Agritech entrepreneurs in live interviews, sharing their experiences, adventures, philosophies, challenges, and insights into their innovative products and businesses.

He is the Executive Director of Positive Impact Africa, an organization devoted to developing and enhancing the performance of youth to make a positive impact in all their endeavors. His past roles include serving as the Managing Director of KrixtoBax Farm Limited, an agro-processing company, and being a member of the board of directors at EyesofAfrika Tv, a platform celebrating the value of Africa.

Kenneth is also associated with the Boardroom Institute and is a fellow of the African Young Leaders Fellowship Program. He is a fellow of the Institute of Management Consultants in Nigeria.

In 2020, he was awarded a scholarship by Agripreneurship Alliance to study Entrepreneurship in Agribusiness at the African Management Institute, Kenya. His accolades include winning the Entrepreneur of the Year (Class of Elite, 2019) from Benson Idahosa University and Young

Entrepreneur of the Year (2019) from The Entrepreneur Africa.

He has received various awards and nominations, including being recognised under the Agriculture category of SME100 Africa's 25 under 25 Nigeria's Enterprising Youth. His brand was honored by Social Good Awards Africa, and he has been featured in entrepreneurship blogs and articles as a rising entrepreneur in Nigeria.

Kenneth was nominated under the Agriculture Category of Africa Youth Award and Entrepreneur of the Year by All Varieties Award. In 2021, he was nominated as Agripreneur of the Year by Founders of the Year Award, Africa, and he clinched the Agriculture award category at Nigeria Achievers Award.

In 2023, Kenneth received the Certificate of Excellence in Educational Engagement from the Office of the Pro Vice-Chancellor of the Royal Agricultural University.

He is an ambassador for The NextGen Agriculture Impact Network (NGIN) and a former ambassador for the UK-based organization, TheirsWorld. Kenneth is also the Convener of "Africa Farmers Convention," one of the largest agro conferences. He serves as the Executive Director of Africa Chambers of Smallholder Farmers, Africa Start-up Forum, and Africa Farmers Network.

Furthermore, he holds the position of National Director, International Association of Agriculture Students and Related Sciences (IAAS), UK Chapter. Recently, he was appointed as the Chair of the Food Security Think Tank under the Food and Agricultural Youth Institute (FAYI).

Kenneth earned his bachelor's degree in Agricultural Economics from Benson Idahosa University and completed a mini-executive MBA in leadership and management at the Accra Business School. He is currently pursuing a master's degree program in Sustainable Agriculture and Food Security at the Royal Agricultural University, United Kingdom.

Kenneth is an alumnus of Fate Foundation and the Enterprise Development Centre (EDC) at Pan Africa University. He has been featured on various television, radio, and podcast platforms, and in numerous blogs, where he shares his expertise on agriculture and agribusiness.

Beyond his professional pursuits, Kenneth is a self-development enthusiast, a captivating conference speaker, and an accomplished writer. He is happily married to his beloved wife, Rose-Helen Obayuwana.

Printed in Great Britain
by Amazon

45051443R00101